Faces in the Voi

Both artists use their craft to create clarity and veracity, and the viewer's experience is very unusual – bearing witness, often to new facts, but represented using beauty, refinement and finely crafted poetry and photography.
Jack Shuttleworth, Project Officer, Herbert Museum, Coventry

The act of writing poetry is itself an act of remembrance ... In the dark space of extinguished lights, each poem illuminates a piece of the shattered world and rescues [it] for the future ...'
Daniel Libeskind

Damaged Czech Sefer Torah, now in the Memorial Scrolls Trust, London.

FACES IN THE VOID

POEMS
by Jane Liddell-King

PHOTOGRAPHS
by Marion Davies

SHAUN TYAS
DONINGTON
2012

.

Published by
SHAUN TYAS
1 High Street
DONINGTON
PE11 4TA

ISBN
978-1-907730-11-5

Printed and bound in Great Britain by
the Lavenham Press Ltd, Lavenham, Suffolk

CONTENTS

FOREWORD

The opening lines of The Bible state that in the beginning, when God created heaven and earth, "the earth was without form and void". There are, of course, many wise rabbinic interpretations of 'formlessness' and 'the void'. And yet, possibly because they unleash our primordial fears that our lives, brief as they are, would be condemned, in effect, to nothingness the moment they are transmuted back to dust, these concepts continue to terrify us. I imagine every one of us combats this terror in his/her own very personal way. The artist's way, I would surmise, has been the conviction that for any creator, perhaps even for God, the void, impenetrable by definition, is not a realm where creation can occur. As many psychoanalytic studies astutely imply, creation is the act of giving form and substance to what already exists even if that existence, like nebulae, exists in a diffused and random agitation.

The above considerations do not mean that I reject the concept of 'voids'. They roam nebulously in our minds and await creation – but not by supernatural forces. We, humankind, create them; and we have created them since time immemorial.

Why do we create them? Simply because we – and by 'we' I mean all humankind – have been indoctrinated, throughout our histories, always to relinquish life in the service of death, for any cause that is arbitrarily designated as 'just'. In effect, we have become worshippers of death instead of worshippers of life. As Robert Oppenheimer wrote: "I am become death, destroyer of worlds". So we have become.

Take a look at any part of the world and you will see that where and when there have been attempts to blanket the earth with voids – attempts that are still ongoing – the authors of these attempts have always been monstrous tyrants and/or cabals that have fomented strife in pursuit of power and supremacy by exploiting racial, political, religious or ideological divides.

The most malevolent attempt to create a void in modern times was conceived by Nazi Germany during Adolf Hitler's Third Reich. This regime, adhering to an abominable ideology, sought to institute, in a perverse echo of Genesis, a new world where a super race, ruled by new super-gods, would keep the earth in thrall for millennia. The Nazis' abominable deeds, particularly their policies of extermination of those peoples they classified as *untermensch*, notably the Jews, the Gypsies and such undesirables as homosexuals, the infirm and political opponents, are well known and need no further elaboration.

Some might say they almost succeeded, that in so far as the European Jews were concerned, they came close to accomplishing annihilation. They didn't. They couldn't have. What tyrants and power-hungry cabals always forget is that the very core of humankind's spirit, the place where our ethical selves reside, will resist the creation of voids in prodigious ways. As Gershom Sholem, quoting the great German-Jewish philosopher, Walter Benjamin, reminds us "I [we, our ethical selves, can always] pluck flowers from the edge of subsistence". Thus the void can never close on itself hermetically to become truly void; thus faces that have fallen into the abyss somehow emerge and, somehow plucking "flowers from the edge of subsistence", give us the hope that the God we love is still the God who endorses the highest moral aspirations that exist in all humankind, and still the God who will transform the world into a paradise liberated from the wholesale killing of peoples.

This remarkable book by Jane Liddell-King and Marion Davies is enriched by faces, by lost lives and by lost and found artefacts that have surfaced from the void the Nazis sought to create. Equally importantly, the book is crowned, in that noble act of bearing witness, with the exceptional collaboration of Marion Davies and Jane Liddell-King. Marion Davies offers us, in an array of extraordinarily strong yet sensitive photographs, a people that will never die. Jane Liddell-King confirms this truth with stark and haunting poems that have the simplicity of pure literature and are imbued with the humanity of our ethical selves. As a tribute both to the victims of the Holocaust and to their spirit, *Faces in the Void* is an homage to those who, by defying evil, ensure that 'voids' will never secure dominion over humankind.

MORIS FARHI

Sofer (scribe) Bernard Benarroch at work at the Memorial Scrolls Trust, London.

Sefer Torah from Pardubice, on loan from the Memorial Scrolls Trust and now in use by Beth Shalom Synagogue, Cambridge.

INTRODUCTION

Faces in the Void exists because of a single Torah scroll – and a riveting sermon. In December 2005, Melissa Lane, then a fellow member of Beth Shalom Reform Synagogue, Cambridge, U.K., addressed the congregation about 'our' scroll. Before the Second World War, the scroll had been owned by a synagogue in Pardubice, a town east of Prague, now in the Czech Republic. At the time 1,256 Jews lived in the region where their ancestors had settled following their expulsion from Spain in 1492.

On 3rd December, 1942, 650 Jews from the Pardubice region and fifty-five neighbouring towns were deported to the Terezín Ghetto, a concentration and transit camp, known in German as Theresienstadt. Four days later a second transport had taken the remaining 606. By the end of the war, only thirty-nine of the deportees were still alive, and just twenty-four from the city of Pardubice itself.

As Melissa spoke, I began to feel impelled to go to Pardubice in search of survivors of the Holocaust (and of Communism). The more I thought about this in the days following, the more I hoped that photographer, Marion Davies would join me. Her exhibition on the Holocaust, 'Absence and Loss, Holocaust Memorials in Berlin and Beyond' (now also a book), had just been launched in Cambridge and the pictures had deeply impressed me. In addition, the New North London Synagogue, to which Marion belongs, also uses a scroll once owned by a Czech community, unidentified, in this case, exterminated in the Holocaust.

Happily, Marion agreed. I felt that we could work independently within our chosen media. Marion would not illustrate my poems and I would not describe her images. Our individual artefacts would complement each other.

Commissioned by my synagogue to uncover the story behind the scroll, Marion and I spent part of the summers of 2006 and 2007 in the Czech Republic. A succession of unexpected and invariably rich encounters rapidly clarified the early life of the scroll.

We arrived in Prague with the daunting warning that there were no longer any living survivors in Pardubice. Within hours, a visit to Iren Ravelová, a Terezín survivor corrected this view.

Leafing through an old address book, she found the details of two fellow survivors from Pardubice. A few days later, Eliška and Jiří met us at Pardubice station and proved to be the first of several survivors who willingly shared

1

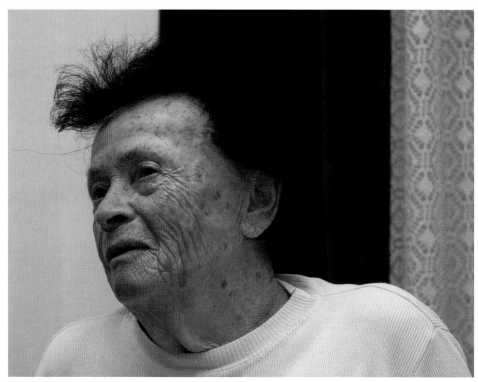

Iren Ravelová.

Eliška Levinská and Jiří Schreiber.

Town square, Pardubice.

Pardubice Synagogue, built 1879–80 and demolished 1958–9.

Site of the Pardubice Synagogue today.

The memorial plaque to Pardubice Synagogue, and in its barely noticeable context.

their unique stories. All of these people had held onto their Jewish identity despite the war years and the Communist régime.

Erected in central Pardubice between 1879 and 1880, the synagogue was reconstructed in 1904. Sited at the corner of a busy intersection, in 1945 it was returned to the Jewish community from whom it had been taken during the Holocaust. Later it became a municipal art gallery. Between 1958 and 1959, it was demolished to make way for urban development. The barely noticeable memorial plaque, erected on the site in 1992 by the Jewish community of Prague, is the only evidence that now remains of a former Jewish place of worship.

In Pardubice, Eliška drove us to the cemetery where Josef was waiting with the key.

While Eliška was talking to Marion, Josef heard me speaking in German. Seizing my arm, he led me to his father's grave, where he later chose to be photographed. He was born in 1941 to a Jewish father and a gentile mother, and had grown up with a deep sense of loss. Shortly after the birth of his sister, Jana, in 1942, Josef's mother divorced Jirí, her husband, and took both her children to the safety of her father's farm in the Bohemian-Moravian mountains. Shortly after that, Jirí killed himself.

The poem, 'Blue Angel' grew out of my first meeting with Josef and subsequent conversations with his daughter, Ester. When she was 16 she had

5

Josef Kraus outside the Ceremonial Hall in Pardubice Jewish cemetery.

asked her father why he had given her such an unusual name. His answer, the revelation of her Jewish roots, prompted her to come to London to read Jewish Studies at University College.

In April 2007, Ester came to Cambridge for the Yom HaShoah (Jewish Holocaust Memorial Day) service at Beth Shalom Synagogue. During the service, she read the list of names of victims from Pardubice murdered in the Holocaust.

The names of all 80,000 Jewish Holocaust victims from Bohemia and Moravia today fill the walls of the Pinkas Synagogue, which is now part of the Jewish museum of Prague, and is dedicated to their memory. Painters Václav Bostik and Jiří John completed this memorial in 1959. In 1968, severe dilapidation forced the closure of the building. Only when the Communist régime fell was the synagogue renovated and reopened in 1996 as part of the Prague Jewish Museum.

While Josef and I were standing at his father's grave, Eliška had been showing Marion the Holocaust monument and the small ceremonial hall where many photographs from the time of her childhood are kept.

Soběchruhy cemetery, dating to approximately 1669, which is being restored by members of the nearby Teplice Jewish community.

Old gravestones placed along the wall of Pardubice cemetery.

Ester Krausová reading from the Torah Scroll from Pardubice
on Yom HaShoah, 2007, Cambridge.
(Opposite) Pinkas Synagogue, Prague, Pardubice victims of the Holocaust
Photo taken with kind permission of The Jewish Museum, Prague

REGINA 27.II 1880 - 6.IX 1943 ADLER BOHUMIL 20.III 1883 - 23.I 1943 PAVLA 11.VI 1889 - 23.I 1943 OLGA 15.VIII 1879 - 6.IX 1943 BÁR OTA 29.VII 1861 - 26.IV 1943 BAUER PAVEL 30.VI 1886 - 18.XII 1943 AUGUSTA 22.IX 1892 - 18.XII 1943 BECKMANNOVÁ ALŽBĚTA 10.X 1887 - 23.I 1943 BENDOVÁ PAVLA 17.V 1880 - 6.IX 1943 BERGMANNOVÁ HEDVIKA 22.IV 1885 - 23.I 1943 KAMILA 12.II 1878 - 6.IX 1943 ALŽBĚTA 23.VII 1894 - 6.IX 1943 BLOCH JOSEF 23.X 1878 - 14.XI 1943 BOHM ADOLF 22.XII 1900 - 22.VI 1942 BONDY MAX 18.II 1877 - 6.IV 1944 BLANKA 1.XII 1898 - 12.X 1944 REGINA 31.I 1862 - 6.III 1943 OT ILIE 6.VII 1884 - 23.I 1943 BRUNNER ARNOŠT 25.IV 1895 - 23.I 1943 JOSEFINA 19.II 1896 - 23.I 1943 JIŘÍ 6.XI 1927 - 23.I 1943 CZERNÁ RŮŽENA 17.XII 1865 - 15.VII 1943 DEIMEL EVŽEN 10.I 1882 - 6.IX 1943 EICHENBAUM ADOLF 10.VI 1882 - 6.IX 1943 IRMA 5.XII 1891 - 6.IX 1943 OTA 11.VI 1925 - 6.IX 1943 EISNEROVÁ KAROLÍNA 1.III 1857 - 13.XII 1943 ENGELMANN KAREL 14.III 1898 - 6.IX 1943 JOSEFINA 19.IX 1905 - 6.IX 1943 JIŘÍ 9.VI 1927 - 6.IX 1943 ENGLÄNDEROVÁ IRMA 6.III 1892 12.X 1944 KAROLÍNA 18.II 1881 - 26.I 1943 OTA 1.VII 1923 - 29.IX 1944 FANTOVÁ ARNOŠTKA 16.III 1875 - 26.I 1943 FEDERER KAREL 31.V 1892 - 18.V 1944 MARTA 18.IX 1906 - 18.V 1944 FEIGLOVÁ HELENA 10.VII 1880 - 6.IX 1943 FELICIE 30.IX 1906 - 23.I 1943 ARNOLD 28.IV 1909 - 23.I 1943 FINKOVÁ MARTA 6.XII 1893 - 17.I 1944 FLEISCHNER HUGO 24.V 1875 - 17.VI 1943 KAROLÍNA 14.XI 1878 - 18.XII 1943 ALŽBĚTA 18.IV 1868 - 19.X 1942 ISIDOR 25.VIII 1868 - 15.XII 1943 MARTA 26.II 1881 - 15.XII 1943 FRANKLOVÁ ELIŠKA 7.IV 1888 23.I 1943 LUCIE 13.XII 1915 - 23.I 1943 FREUND JINDŘICH 29.II 1877 - 15.XII 1943 JULIE 8.VII 1879 - 15.XII 1943 RUDOLF 4.II 1910 - 23.I 1943 VĚRA 17.X 1917 - 6.IX 1943 JOSEF 25.XI 1890 - 28.IX 1944 KAREL 12.IV 1920 - 1.X 1944 EVA 22.III 1930 - 19.X 1944 TEREZIE 30.V 1859 - 1.III 1943 FRIEDMANN KAREL 8.VII 1891 - 18.V 1944 ZDEŇKA 15.II 1889 - 18.V 1944 MILAN 30.V 1926 - 18.V 1944 MARTIN 22.VII 1859 - 24.VII 1943 RŮŽENA 18.VIII 1888 - 23.I 1943 EMIL 17.VIII 1886 - 23.I 1943 MARTA 9.V 1893 - 23.I 1943 JIŘÍ 9.V 1919 - 23.I 1943 HANA 9.V 1919 - 23.I 1943 FUCHS ROBERT 4.VII 1894 - 23.I 1943 MILADA 12.II 1899 - 23.I 1943 JAROSLAV 22.VII 1914 - 23.I 1943 GETREUER HUGO 9.IX 1882 - 6.IX 1943 SELMA 16.X 1892 - 6.IX 1943 GLASER EMIL 29.VIII 1888 - 23.I 1943 MARIE 18.V 1896 - 6.IX 1943 ERIKA 14.IV 1926 - 6.IX 1943 KAMILA 10.II 1928 - 6.IX 1943 GLÜCKNER VIKTOR 2.XII 1876 - 15.XII 1943 HEDVIKA 4.IV 1882 - 15.XII 1943 GOLDREICH EMIL 28.III 1874 - 15.XII 1943 ANNA 13.III 1885 - 15.XII 1943 ROBERT 9.XI 1911 - 6.IX 1943 GOTTLIEB BEDŘICH 24.X 1901 - 23.I 1943 RUDOLF 31.X 1909 - 23.I 1943 HANA 14.I 1921 - 23.I 1943 GROSMANOVÁ MARIE 9.VII 1894 - 23.I 1943 BERTA 5.V 1896 - 23.I 1943 BERNÁT 27.III 1902 - 23.I 1943 GROTTE ALFRED 19.VII 1903 - 23.I 1943 KAREL 2.VIII 1900 - 23.I 1943 OLGA 28.IV 1899 - 23.I 1943 MILADA 26.IV 1930 - 23.I 1943 HANA 8.XI 1930 - 23.I 1943 PAVEL 30.VIII 1936 - 23.I 1943 ANNA 8.V 1863 - 18.IV 1943 HARPUDER SAMUEL 8.V 1889 - 6.XI 1943 JINDŘIŠKA 29.VI 1890 - 6.XI 1943 HEISLEROVÁ JULIE 22.III 1886 - 20.I 1943 HANA 17.X 1916 - 20.I 1943 HERRMANN JOSEF 4.VII 1915 - 6.IX 1943 HERTA 11.III 1919 - 6.IX 1943 OTA 19.II 1910 - 20.I 1943 HOCH OTILIE 30.V 1892 - 16.X 1944 HANA 1.III 1922 - 16.X 1944 MARGITA 5.I 1925 - 16.X 1944 HUGO 2.IX 1883 - 6.IX 1943 ANNA 7.X 1884 - 6.IX 1943 KAREL 4.V 1912 - 12.VII 1943 ROBERT 31.X 1887 - 23.IV 1943 IRMA 4.VI 1885 - 30.VIII 1943 HOCHMANN ALOIS 12.IV 1865 - 31.III 1943 MILADA 23.X 1874 - 15.XII 1943 ZDEŇKA 25.V 1899 - 23.I 1943 RŮŽENA 2.III 1901 - 23.I 1943 OTA 7.IX 1910 - 8.II 1945 OTA 12.V 1895 - 23.I 1943 OLGA 20.XI 1894 - 23.I 1943 JIŘÍ 19.VI 1921 - 23.I 1943 ALBERT 30.IV 1928 - 23.I 1943 MARIE 13.II 1897 - 23.I 1943 KAREL 11.X 1922 - 23.I 1943 VĚRA 12.XI 1923 - 23.I 1943 MARIE 15.II 1923 - 4.X 1944 SYLVA RUTH 13.IV 1943 - 4.X 1944 HUMBURGEROVÁ TEREZIE 6.VII 1887 - 15.XII 1943 GUSTAV 22.XII 1915 - 15.XII 1943 JELINKOVÁ IDA 4.MARIE 7.III 1885 - 23.I 1943 KAČER RICHARD 23.VI 1879 - 26.XII 1942 IDA 8.VII 1892 - 23.I 1943 HELENA 27.VIII 1925 - 23.I 1943 KAFKA PAVEL 5.IV 1889 - 26.I 1943 MARTA 14.XI 1900 - 26.I 1943 KAREL 22.V 1922 - 26.I 1943 NORA 20.VIII 1928 - 26.I 1943 RUDOLF 17.VI 1885 - 23.I 1943 GABRIELA 2.XII 1890 - 23.I 1943 KAUDERSOVÁ OLGA 16.VII 1915 - 23.I 1943 KAUFMANN LEO 6.II 1889 - 28.X 1944 KATZ OTA 16.II 1880 - 6.IX 1943 IDA 8.IV 1885 - 6.IX 1943 KLATSCHEROVÁ AMÁLIE 28.IV 1872 - 18.V 1944 ARNOŠTKA 10.II 1905 - 15.XII 1943 ALENA 16.III 1936 - 15.XII 1943 KLAUBAUF EMIL 23.II 1907 - 28.IV 1944 VILMA 6.III 1912 - ALENA 10.V 1934 - 6.XI 1944 VA 7.III 1937 - 6.XI 1944 HANA 13.XII 1941 6.XI 1944 KLEIN ARNOŠT 13.IV 1892 - 23.I 1943 EMILIE 11.V 1899 - 23.I 1943 EGON 14.V 1925 - 23.I 1943 EVA 11.II 1938 - 23.I 1943 OTA 15.VIII 1885 - 29.IV 1943 ANNA 29.II 1896 - 6.IX 1943 PAVEL 11.VII 1928 - 6.IX 1943 EDITA 12.V 1913 - 23.I 1943 KOHN ALFRED 23.IV 1874 - 15.XII 1943 BEDŘICH 17.X 1870 - 11.V 1943 ROLF 6.XII 1877 - 15.XII 1943 VALTR 4.IX 1907 - 23.I 1943 KOPPERLOVÁ MARTA 12.VIII 1901 - 6.IX 1943 EVA 18.IV 1929 - 6.IX 1943 KRÁSA VÍTĚZSLAV 5.VI 1881 - 19.X 1944 MARIE 17.III 1882 - 30.IX 1944 JARMILA 9.V 1920 - 12.X 1944 EMILIE 30.VIII 1877 - 15.XII 1943 KRAUS MAX 16.III 1882 - 6.IX 1943 IRMA 20.XII 1885 - 6.IX 1943 KUMPEROVÁ ŠTĚPÁNKA 5.XI 1906 - 23.X 1944 LAMPLOVÁ MARIE 14.VI 1870 - 12.III 1943 LEDERER EMIL 14.V 1911 - 24.VIII 1942 ROBERT 7.XII 1870 - 20.I 1943 EMILIE 12.XII 1878 - 6.IX 1943 LIEBERMANNOVÁ ELKA 10.V 1912 - 23.I 1943 LÖFFLER BEDŘICH 22.VI 1913 - 23.I 1943 LOEWY KAREL 10.XII 1881 - 26.X 1942 VELYNA 2.VII 1928 - 6.IX 1943 LOWY VIKTOR 20.III 1885 - 23.I 1943 MARTA 26.XI 1888 - 23.I 1943 LUSTIG LEOPOLD 16.II 1892 - 23.I 1943 OTA 16.XI 1896 - 8.II 1945 LEONORA 27.II 1904 - 23.I 1943 MANDELIKOVÁ FRANTIŠKA 1.IV 1865 - 24.II 1943 MOSCHELOVÁ IRMA 16.VIII 1891 - 12.X 1942 MÜLLEROVÁ JOSEFINA 8.III 1887 - 6.IX 1943 MATYLDA 10.V 1883 - 23.I 1943 OLGA 16.V 1884 - 23.I 1943 MUNK KAREL 23.II 1895 - 1.X 1944 HERMÍNA 18.II 1905 - 12.X 1944 RŮŽENA 15.VIII 1867 - 15.XII 1943 NETTL RUDOLF 11.X 1885 - 26.I 1943 GERTRUDA 14.V 1891 - 26.I 1943 VILÉM 12.III 1924 - 26.I 1943 JIŘÍ 28.XII 1926 - 26.I 1943 NEUMANN FRANTIŠEK 8.II 1899 - 6.IX 1943 TRUDA 22.III 1914 - 6.IX 1943 HUGO 7.III 1876 - 23.I 1943 MARIE 7.XII 1893 - 6.IX 1943 OTA 13.XI 1879 - 6.IX 1943 JULIUS 30.IX 1887 - 23.I 1943 PAVLA 21.V 1887 - 23.I 1943 OESTERREICHER BENO 10.VI 1896 - 23.I 1943 BERTA 24.II 1862 - 21.III 1943 HYNEK 9.VI 1867 - 27.I 1943 JULIE 1.VIII 1873 - 15.XII 1943 PAVEL 20.V 1894 - 6.IX 1943 MARKÉTA 14.VII 1892 - 20.I 1943 PACHNEROVÁ EVA 29.II 1935 - 6.IX 1943 PICK OSKAR 3.VII 1893 - 1.III 1943 IRENA 16.V 1894 - ANNA 3.II 1943 - 23.I 1943 ANNA 22.VII 1902 - 23.I 1943 FRANTIŠKA 22.V 1849 - 22.XII 1942 PIRAK KAREL 18.III 1886 - 23.I 1943 BERTA 27.VII 1893 - 23.I 1943 OTA 26.IX 1928 - 23.I 1943 POLLAK JOSEF 7.VII 1878 - 6.IX 1943 JOSEF 25.VII 1898 23.II 1943 LEOPOLD 28.III 1908 - 28.X 1944 ZUZANA 29.VII 1936 - 28.X 1944 JANA 3.V 1944 - PAVEL 16.IV 1916 - 7.II 1945 AUGUSTA 17.VII 1884 - 6.IX 1943 IRENA 1.V 1907 - 18.V 1944 LEA LENKA 21.III 1930 - 19.V 1944 JOSEF EDVARD 27.I 1935 - 18.V 1944 POPPER EMIL 11.II 1897 - 23.I 1943 JAROSLAVA 25.X 1900 - 23.I 1943 VĚRA 3.I 1926 - 23.I 1943 OTA 29.XII 1920 - 23.I 1943 EMIL 18.III 1905 - 6.IX 1943 CHARLOTA 22.VII 1907 - 23.I 1943 FLORA 20.II 1866 - 15.XII 1943 JIŘÍ 17.IV 1915 - 23.I 1943 PAVLÍNA 9.XII 1873 - 31.VII 1943 RICHARD 26.IX 1898 - 26.II 1943 ALFRED 10.II 1906 - 23.I 1943 RAIS JINDŘICH 30.VII 1895 - 23.III 1943 RAUCHER ISIDOR 11.II 1865 - 21.X 1943 ARNOŠTKA 29.XII 1871 - 15.XII 1943 KAREL 3.XII 1906 - 23.I 1943 REDLICHOVÁ GRÉTA 29.VII 1910 - 15.XII 1943 VA 22.IV 1943 - 15.XII 1943 REICHMANN DAVID 10.X 1895 - 6.IX 1943 OTAKAR 14.XII 1909 - 23.I 1943 ZDEŇKA 24.IV 1917 - 23.I 1943 BERTA 16.V 1876 - 15.XII 1943 HANA 11.VIII 1927 - 19.X 1944 RIES KAREL 29.VII 1896 - 20.I 1943 EVA 1.II 1866 - 22.V 1943 ROBITSCHKOVÁ ANEŽKA 1.II 1879 - 6.IX 1943 HANA 17.VIII 1908 - 6.IX 1943 ROSEN RICHARD 17.II 1882 - 24.V 1943 JANA 24.VI 1892 - 21.X 1943 ROSTEINSKÁ BERTA 20.X 1903 - 23.I 1943 ROURICKOVÁ MARIE 19.XII 1942 - 4.X 1944 RŮŽENA 10.II 1878 - 18.XII 1943 ALŽBĚTA 10.X 1905 - 6.IX 1943

Cemetery Ceremonial Hall, interior, Pardubice Jewish cemetery.

All this time, Jiří had been standing quietly in the background waiting to talk. Eventually, he explained he had to return home to his sick wife. This did not deter him from beginning a remarkable story which, over many months, unfolded by telephone and letter, and prompted me to write 'The Pious Place at the River Ohře'. This place is now a memorial site to a terrible event.

From the beginning of November 1944, the Nazis tried to erase all evidence of their atrocities in Terezín. Thirty-thousand burial boxes from the Columbarium containing the remains of individual men, women and children were to be emptied into the nearby river. In the morning, child inmates were forced to pass the boxes containing the ashes from the urn chamber to waiting trucks. Later, prisoners over sixty-five took over. A pontoon bridge was quickly built to help with the disposal of the ashes of the dead.

When Jiří had left and Josef had locked the cemetery, Eliška took us to lunch in the town centre. Her childhood unfolded in story after story and picture after picture. The poem 'Skin' grew out of Eliška's recollections. And then her mobile rang: "That was Ladislav. He wanted to remind me – as if I might forget – that his mother was one of twins experimented on by Mengele. But he won't speak to you".

Naturally, we had to meet the elusive Ladislav. A year and much

Columbarium, Terezín.

The Pious Place Memorial, Terezín.

persuasion later, we finally did. A morning spent with him prompted the poem, 'Family Tree'.

When Marion, Eliška and I went into his downtown bar and *penzion*, he was in the bar playing a video of his family in Israel with the Hatikvah as background music. As we talked – haltingly at first with the help of Eliška's translations, and then more fluently in German and Hebrew, Ladislav gradually went back over his life. He left the room and returned with pictures of his mother, his family, a handful of 'ghetto geld' and pre-war post-cards, each adding to his family history, and his carefully researched family tree. There was no need to question him. We had only to listen. As he confided in us, he revealed the profound loneliness of a Jew without a community.

During our visit, I stayed with Eliška in Pardubice. She spoiled me with her cooking: plums, cheese, potatoes, awed me with her energy and resourcefulness, epitomised by the swimsuit and pair of climbing boots kept at the ready in her car, and she humbled me with her optimism and endless capacity to adapt, to go on. Terézia kindly drove her grandmother, Marion and me to places of Jewish interest. First, we visited Dřevíkov, a tiny village to the south of Pardubice. Typifying Jewish life as it once was, the village has only one street, still known as the Jewish Street, and dating from the mid-eighteenth

Herta Weiss (22 February 1906–
March 1976, Pardubice), and
Erwin Weiss (12 February 1894–
28 October 1944, Auschwitz).

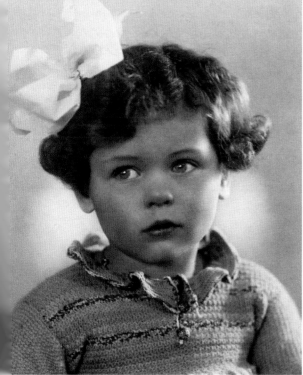

Eliška Levinská née Weiss,
daughter of the above.

(opposite) "I am the last Jew", Ladislav Novák behind the bar in his small hotel, Penzion 2727, Pardubice.

(left) The home of Ladislav Novák's great-grandparents in Chvojno.

Hana Seinerová and Milan Seiner (twins, born 16 November 1933).

Hana Seinerová together with her family in Israel after 1945.

Židovská Ulička (Jewish Street), Drevíkov.

century when Jews had formed the majority of the population. Standing outside the house where she was born, 100-year-old Boýena pointed out a white building at the end of the street, originally the synagogue. A wooden building, Number 47, Židovská Ulička, had once been a small distillery and later a bakery. Boýena's own house had been the Jewish hospital and then the Jewish school, which closed in the 1860s.

The poem, 'Damals', begins with Boýena's memories.

Later that day, Eliška took us to the chilling perfection of the restored synagogue in the nearby village of Heřmanův Městec, a few kilometers north of Dřevíkov. Now there is no Jewish community; instead, the building has become a museum and concert hall. In 2006, a mikveh (a bath for ritual purification) was found, possibly medieval – and in a damaged state. I tried to put both the acute sense of loss and a moment's hopefulness into the poem.

Heřmanův Městec had been a home to Jews for 500 years. By the end of the fifteenth century, they had their own synagogue and cemetery. The present synagogue, built originally in 1870, replaced one from 1728. It stands prominently in the centre of the former ghetto. In 1848 there had been a population of 840 Jews. That had fallen to a mere fifty-four by 1930. After the Second World War, only six Jews returned. Their synagogue became an

Eliška Levinská with her grand-daughter, Terézia.

בואו שעריו בתורח הצרתיו בהחלה
הזוזו לי גרבו שמו למק

Synagogue, Heřmanův Městec.

Heřmanův Městec, detail above Aron Hakodesh (Ark).

Evangelical Church and then a warehouse. And then, in the late 1990s it was restored to its full architectural glory. The Aron Hakodesh (Ark), in which the Torah scrolls are kept, was preserved from the original building. The women prayed separately, upstairs in the gallery. They entered the synagogue over a bridge through a connecting house, home to the Rabbi, and also accommodating the school, which was built in 1859.

Now, Terézia is following in her grandmother's footsteps and learning to be a guide at Terezín, to keep her grandmother's story alive.

In September 2009, Eliška and I exchanged e-mails. Hers to me reads:

> I like to say you hello. And I like to ask you if you know about the Winton train, it's leaving yesterday Prague to London? Mr Sir Nicholas Winton is a man from England and he saved 669 children from the Czech Republic in the year 1938–1939. The survivors their families and some students were invited to Prague

Alice Sommer-Herz.

and the train started from the same railway station and is using the same way to London, where Sir Nicholas Winton is waiting, he is 100 years old. Yesterday our TV was sending the whole day the information about the train and this morning the train is in Koln-Germany. It is arriving on September 4th in London.

I hope you are well, the same as I am in this time.

The best from Eliška.

When we returned to the UK, our project acquired new contributors, including Sir Nicholas Winton. But first Alice Sommer-Herz added her own unique chapter to our Czech Jewish story. In 2006, when we first met her, she was 103. She had lived in North London since leaving Israel when her twin sister Marianne died aged 77. "Marianne died young," she explained, "because she was a pessimist. Even as a child she was always anxious. Once she disappeared. Mother was frantic. Marianne thought she was ill and had taken herself to the doctor. She was seven years old."

Born into a family to whom culture, and music in particular, was of crucial importance, Alice had a successful career as a pianist. Her mother had played piano duets with Mahler, and Alice remembers Kafka's many visits to

Franz Kafka Monument, Prague, by Jaroslav Róna.

the family home. Typically, within days of their first meeting, Alice decided to marry her husband-to-be because, as a very young man, he had written the most touching and thoughtful condolence letter following the death from 'flu of a close friend. "He used words perfectly and he was a fine violinist." She remembers their going to a concert during her pregnancy. As the musicians played, her unborn son, with perfect timing, kicked the programme from her lap.

As a 6-year-old newcomer to Terezín in 1943, that child, her son Stefan, was chosen for the part of the sparrow in Hans Krása's children's opera *Brundibár*. The opera was performed fifty-five times in the Magdeburg barracks in Terezín, but the cast changed constantly as children were routinely deported to Auschwitz. Among a tiny number of child survivors, Alice's son later became the internationally acclaimed cellist, Raphael Sommer. Sadly, he died aged only sixty-five in 2001.

In Terezín, sitting with other musicians, Alice worked in the mica factory. "It was an ordeal to sit for eight hours, in the cold, and separate out the mica into thin pieces." These slices of the mineral were used in electronic equipment. Later she was employed to wash linen and had to get up at 4.00 am. Leaving her son at such an hour was a daily agony. But music and the fact of sharing a mattress kept them alive. During her time in Terezín, Alice gave 100 concerts, which included the full cycle of Chopin's *Études*. Her husband was deported to Auschwitz, where he died. Music can be said to have saved Alice's life, as a Nazi guard who had heard her play promised her she would not follow her husband.

Her stories prompted the poem, 'Appassionata'. This was the second poem I wrote for Alice. The first poem, 'Gedenkstätte', was the very first of all the poems that I wrote. If it seems to relate obliquely to the rest, it reflects the very difficulty of making a start. I didn't feel able to plunge straight into testimony. With just days to go before the first presentation for Jewish Holocaust Memorial Day, one image haunted me: Gedenkstätte beside the River Ohře near Terezín. As I gazed at Marion's photograph of this river (page 76) a few clear thoughts came to mind. Gedenkstätte means a place of thoughtfulness, of recollection. Such sites can be found throughout Europe, marking particular events of the Holocaust.

Marion's picture showed the sheer beauty of the river. There seemed no point in trying to put this into words. And, as it was, I couldn't forget the ashes of the dead beneath the surface, nor how, paradoxically, only a few miles upstream, Alice's cherished composer, Beethoven, had visited Karlsbad at a critical moment in his life, to take the healing waters. Now, curative minerals

Poster for *Brundibár*, a Children's Opera by Hans Krása, reproduced with kind permission of Terezín Memorial, Hermann's collection, © Zuzana Dvořáková.

22

I.

L. v. Beethoven	:	Apasionata
Bach-Patita	:	B Dur
Chopin	:	Etuden

II.

L. v. Beethoven	:	Sonate Op. 81
V. Ullmann	:	Sonate
C. Debussy	:	Refec dans l'eau
"	:	Ministrels
R. Schuhmann	:	Karneval

III.

J. Brahms	:	Intermezzi
"	:	Rhapsodie G moll
R. Schuhmann	:	Symph. Etuden

IV.

L.v. Beethoven	:	Sonate D Dur Op 10
R. Schuhmann	:	Fantasie
B. Smetana	:	Tänze

Alice Sommer-Herz's Concert Programme, reproduced with kind permission of Terezín Memorial, Hermann's collection, © Zuzana Dvořáková.

mingled with the ashes of Jewish dead. Despite Beethoven's emotional trauma, his Eighth Symphony had come to mind. Eventually, this initial poem came out of these thoughts, and the remarkable fact that Marion and I have been able to bear witness.

In May 2008, we had met the then 99-year-old Sir Nicholas Winton. Vera Gissing, one of the 669 children whom he had rescued, had introduced us. The day stayed in my mind: Vera's beautiful and isolated cottage, the cows in the neighbouring field which she jokingly called her own; her candour, warmth and endless humour.

Vera, Sir Nicholas, Marion and I lunched in a nearby pub. For the first time in years, I was dumbfounded. I had never met anyone to compare with Sir Nicholas, and I stared fixedly into my soup. Sensing my unease, he leant across the table and beamed: "Share my sausage."

"Only if you share my soup," I heard myself answer. And then we talked. And back in his garden we went on talking. "What is clear," he said, "is that we learn nothing from history. And you, you are a writer, why can't you explain this?"

"All I can do is to go on writing about people in the hope of clearer understanding. After all her suffering, Vera's like champagne," I added.

"Far better," he replied. "She lasts longer. If only governments could

23

(Following pages) Sir Nicholas Winton and Vera Gissing.

Jane Liddell-King and Vera Gissing.

Vera and Eva Diamant photographed soon after their arrival in England.

sustain the will to change for any length of time. I mean to bring about real change focusing on peace and peaceable co-existence, and even justice."

With the Germans already occupying Czechoslovakia in the winter of 1938, instead of going on a skiing holiday, 29-year-old Nicholas Winton had gone to Prague in answer to a call for help from a friend. Responding quickly to the critical situation, he began to organise the Czech Kindertransport. Over nine months, eight trains carried 669 Jewish children to the U.K. where they were safe and could be looked after. Scattered across the world, these children have now produced about 5,000 descendants. Very few of them saw their parents again. In 2002, Sir Nicholas Winton was knighted for his services to humanity. He has been awarded both the Freedom of the City of Prague and the Czech Republic's highest military decoration. In 1998, a planet was named after him.

The poem I eventually wrote for Sir Nicholas and Vera was called 'I speak to the child that I was' because that was how Vera had begun the story she told Marion and me.

Sir Nicholas first met Vera on Esther Rantzen's television show, 'That's Life'. Coming across records in the attic, his wife had determined that his achievements be brought to public notice some fifty years after his journey to Prague. Vera is now his neighbour, biographer and devoted friend. She and her sister Eva left Czechoslovakia on one of his Kinderstransports in June, 1939. They were never to see their parents again. Vera's cousins, Tomas and Honzi had been scheduled to leave on 3 September, 1939, the day the British declared war on Germany. The Germans stopped the train from leaving and nearly all of the 250 children on it subsequently died in the Holocaust. Over tea in his house, Sir Nicholas talked at length about the painful and haunting memory of that last train.

Auschwitz II-Birkenau, where Vera's cousins died, was set up in the spring of 1942 as an extension of Auschwitz Main Camp. New arrivals were selected for forced labour or to be gassed immediately. At peak strength, Birkenau operated four gas chambers. More than 44,000 Jews were deported from Terezín and murdered in Birkenau. Overall, more than two and a half million Jews were deported there and at least two and a quarter million murdered.

Although a Torah scroll unwinds longitudinally, as the Jewish year progresses, no sooner does the story end than it begins again. And so it was with our work.

In January, 2010, 'Faces in the Void' was exhibited at the Herbert Museum in Coventry. During our preparations for this, I went back over the connections between Coventry and Lidice, each of which had suffered so

(Following pages) Auschwitz II-Birkenau, Poland, entrance to the camp opposite the train ramp.

Memorial with plaque which marks the friendship between Coventry and Lidice, Coventry.

deeply. In 1944, Czech President Edvard Beneš attended a memorial service held in the ruins of Coventry Cathedral for the martyred Czech village. On May 8, 1947, Coventry sent representatives to the laying of the foundation stone of the new village of Lidice. In 1972, a square in Coventry was named Lidice Place.

On Wednesday May 27, 1942 Reinhard Heydrich, the vicious Reichsprotektor of Czechoslovakia, was being driven to his office at Prague Castle. His car was attacked by two Czechoslovak resistance fighters, Jozef Gabčík and Jan Kubiš, who had been trained in Britain. Heydrich was fatally wounded and Hitler ordered instant reprisals. The village of Lidice, ten miles northwest of Prague, and the settlement of Lezáky, near Pardubice, were singled out. Acting on information received, the Gestapo focused its attentions on the Pardubice region where SILVER A, a resistance group of key importance to the assassination plot, was based.

By coincidence, at the time of the assassination, two men from the apparently insignificant mining village of Lidice, farmer's son Pilot Officer Josef Horák, and Flight Lieutenant Josef Stříbrný, were serving in the Czechoslovak 311 bomber squadron of the Royal Air Force. Circumstantial evidence convinced the Gestapo that the small village of miners and farmers

Horák Farm Ruins, Lidice

harboured partisans.

In consequence, on 9 and 10 June, 173 innocent men were killed outside Josef Horák's family farm. After the men had been killed, the children were separated from their mothers and taken to the Łódź ghetto. Their mothers were deported to Ravensbrück concentration camp, where most of them died.

Selected children were sent to Germany to be 'Aryanised'. On the orders of Adolf Eichmann, eighty-two were taken to Chełmno and killed in gas vans. By the end of the war, only seventeen children had survived. They eventually returned to find that their entire village had been burned to the ground.

In September 1942, in Great Britain, Barnett Stross, a Jewish, Polish-born doctor, inspired coal miners in Stoke-on-Trent to respond to the devastating fate of their Czech co-workers. Together with other British coal miners, these men founded the organisation 'Lidice Shall Live' to raise funds for the rebuilding of the village after the war. In 1954, Dr Stross, then MP for Stoke-on-Trent, initiated plans for a commemorative rose garden. Coventry contributed to the many thousands of roses sent from across the world. Stross was knighted in 1964.

Aside from these well-documented events, I found another less well-known story. I discovered that, as a member of the Czech Division of the RAF, based near Swindon, Pilot Officer Josef Horák had married a British woman called Winifred New. In 1948 Winifred and her two sons were able to leave Czechoslovakia on a legal passport. Josef had to walk to Vienna from where he eventually returned home to Swindon. He died following an air crash on January 18, 1949. Subsequently, Winifred remarried.

A brief item in the *Swindon Advertiser* led eventually to a glorious afternoon spent in the company of Winifred and her elder son, Josef. Story after story poured from them, and I wanted to devote a whole sequence of poems to Winifred alone. After all, a woman who had contemplated tobogganing from the Czech Republic into Austria with a small son on her knees in order to escape the punitive communist régime was extraordinary enough. In the end, I confined myself to 'Politik' alone.

When I thought I'd finished this introduction, Marion shook her head. "Tomatoes," she kept saying, and "Domov". With her encouragement, I went back to a story that I had found particularly disturbing. The teller, an elderly Terezín survivor, Martin Glas, had spoken in German, to Marion, and I had missed much of his rapid narrative. Born in Prague in June 1931 to a Jewish father, Julian Glas and a non-Jewish mother, Gertrud, German was Martin's first language. The family were deported to Terezín in April 1942, and there separated. Martin was placed in a children's barracks. His father was a keen amateur musician and Martin recalled his singing in the choir in Smetana's *The Bartered Bride*, one of many cultural activities which he believed enabled the Ghetto inmates to preserve *menshlichkeit*: basic human decency and hope. As a member of the Jewish council, Julian was able to secure his wife, who suffered from TB, a job in the fields growing vegetables. Sadly, he was sent to Auschwitz on the very last transport from the Ghetto, and died there. Gertrud survived. Martin himself had edited *Domov*, one of several magazines produced by very young prisoners in their respective barracks. These editors included Petr Ginz. These magazines were a crucial means of asserting independence. As Martin pointed out, minimal education proved no bar to the contributors' creativity.

When Marion translated the parts of Martin's testimony which I had missed, the story of his continuing struggle for acceptance in the Jewish world of Prague moved me so deeply that I hardly felt able to write about it. And then, quite suddenly, months later, 'Tomatophobia' came to me, and the other short poems followed.

Believing our project complete, Marion and I looked back over our work. Key questions were still unanswered and perhaps unanswerable. These ranged from what enabled the survivors we had met to keep going in intolerable circumstances and to remain alert to the sufferings of those around them, to

Winifred New and
Josef Horák.

Martin Glas holding
the map of Terezín
annotated by his
father.

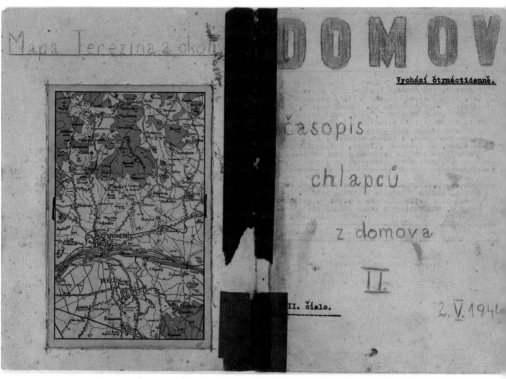

Domov front and back cover, with map of area around Terezín.

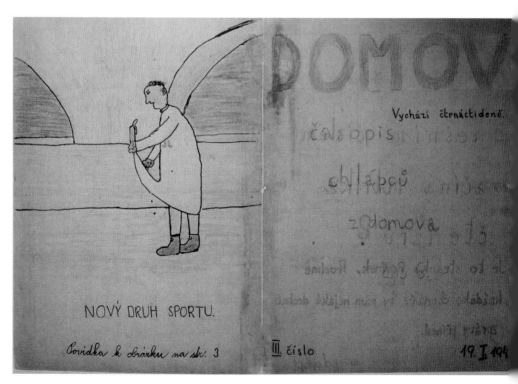

A pair of pages from *Domov*.

what had motivated seemingly ordinary Germans to be beguiled by Hitler's dream of a thousand-year Aryan Reich, to lose all sense of humanity and to participate in the Nazi enterprise of industrialised murder? Underlying these questions was the matter of how we ourselves would behave under similar circumstances.

The many layered testimonies, so compellingly told to us, revealed people in confrontation with the harshest experiences: terror, anguish and humiliation as well as starvation, cold and disease. Unforgettable recollections revealed modes of survival, moments of intimacy, compassion and humour, artistic expression and religious observance, the unexpected discovery of building and engineering skills, all were among the diverse resources on which survivors drew.

Before we left for Prague, an old school friend, Angela Thirlwell, put us in touch with Eva Loukotová whom she had met in Prague on a school trip in the '60s. Eva entertained, guided and encouraged us on both our visits. She introduced us to her mother, Vlasta Fošenbauerová and to her son, Daniel, her daughter-in-law, Miri and her two grandsons, Ron and Eli.

Having married a non-Jew, Eva's mother avoided deportation until late in the War but eventually spent a year in Terezín while her husband was sent to a 'special' labour camp. It was Eva who drove us to Terezín.

Our meetings gave rise to "Family" which I wrote in Jerusalem.

Walking round Terezín we were sharply aware of a town that functioned normally but was dominated by a 'living' museum of torment. The illusion of the *Verschönerung,* the temporary reconstruction of the Ghetto undertaken to dispel the suspicions of the Red Cross when they visited Terezín in June 1944, hung in the air we breathed. In the months leading up to this visit, meticulous cosmetic surgery had been performed to reassure the inspectors that the Ghetto was precisely as claimed: a garrison town adapted to serve the needs of elderly Jews and families.

On 5 October 1943, a transport of some 400 Danish Jews who had failed to escape to Sweden arrived in Terezín. In November, urged on by insistent protests from the King of Denmark and other leading Danish figures, the Swedish and Danish Red Cross asked to visit these new arrivals. Their notorious visit on 23 June 1944 was, in all probability, a propaganda move initiated in May 1943 by Heinrich Himmler, SS chief. This was a perfect opportunity to refute charges of atrocities in the concentration camps and ghettos. With tragic irony, the extreme overcrowding was an awkward but not insurmountable bar to the ultimately desired image. The problem would be solved by deportations to Auschwitz. Of the 39,957 inmates crammed into the

Eva Loukotová outside the nursery in Terezín where her mother, Vlasta Fošenbauerová, worked as a prisoner. The building houses a nursery today.

Prayer room, painted by prisoner Artur Berlinger, used by Danish prisoners, Terezín.

Ghetto in December 1943, 7,500 would have to leave. Terezín was to resemble a happy holiday resort.

As I collected more and more information about Terezín, I wrote about the capacity to survive, and the question of what had motivated Nazi brutality became more and more insistent. I decided to focus on the ghetto's last Kommandant, Karl Rahm. When he took over the command of the Ghetto, in order to graft an image of normality onto the utterly abnormal, he ordered Jewish Elder, Dr Paul Eppstein to arrange for the agonising deportations. The transports included Czechs, Germans, Austrians and Dutch Jews. In case the Red Cross wished to visit these prisoners in Auschwitz, on arrival there they were held in a special camp known as the Theresienstadt Family Camp. In July 1944, once the Red Cross visit was safely over, all of these victims were murdered.

Under the control of Karl Rahm, the Ghetto became the Jewish Settlement Area of Theresienstadt, where leisure and pleasure were emphasised. Rahm oversaw the laying of turf, flower beds, and sand paths. A pavilion for a municipal orchestra was built in a corner of the square. A band played in a café and music hall artists performed regularly. Children were provided with a playground with swings, a glass roofed pavilion and a paddling pool. Indoors, they were given rocking horses, play tables and coloured stools. A sports ground was equipped with showers. The new Sports' Hall housed a community centre including a stage, prayer hall and library.

The hospitals suddenly acquired white sheets, pillows and the nurses were given sparkling uniforms. Furniture was made for the elderly occupants of the lower billets. A large hut served as a Mess Hall where waitresses wearing spotless aprons served much improved food and gave out new cutlery. At the same time, records of deaths were destroyed, parcels were withheld until the day of the visit itself.

Before the actual visit, K. H. Frank, the Nazi official in charge of Bohemia and Minister Moravec, a member of the Czech Quisling government, inspected the improvements.

The day itself was carefully choreographed and rehearsed to the last detail. A bank manger imprisoned for three months for illicit smoking was offered a cigar. Immaculately dressed girls shouldered rakes and marched past the visitors singing. Both Verdi's *Requiem* and Hans Krása's children's opera, *Brundibár* were performed and a football match took place on the sports ground.

Representatives of the Red Cross in Berlin, the Danish foreign minister and representatives of the Scandinavian Red Cross, were completely taken in.

Inexplicably, they failed to inspect the hospitals or home for the elderly. Nor did they ask about the sanitary arrangements. They did not visit the prison in the basement of the Nazi Headquarters. Nor did they ask about the number of deaths.

On 24 June, four artists who, by contrast, had carefully and at great risk, recorded life in the Ghetto as it really was and who had succeeded in smuggling their work out, were brutally interrogated by Adolf Eichmann. Together with their families, Otto Ungar, Bedrich Fritta, Felix Bloch and Leo Haas were sent to the prison in the Small Fortress. Bloch and Fritta were subsequently murdered in Auschwitz. Ungar died of typhus in Buchenwald a month after the camp was liberated. Only Haas survived.

What I wondered, might have prompted Karl Rahm to join the Nazis in the first place and why was he singled out to complete the all-important job of wholesale deception?

Rahm was born in Klosterneuburg, a suburb of Vienna in 1907. Following an elementary school education, he became a toolmaker. Later, he became a Warrant Officer and was commissioned in Bohemia where he gained a medal for special merit. Having worked in Eichmann's office earlier in the war, he was appointed Kommandant of Terezín on 8 February 1944. His behaviour to the prisoners oscillated between violent outbursts and sudden compassionate gestures. These bare facts of his early life drew me inevitably to Vienna, the crucible for the development of the Aryan identity. The cradle of modernity where Freud reinvented the roots of identity, where Theodor Herzl studied law, where Schnitzler mapped a disillusioned world, and where café culture and music had flourished, was invaded by a völkish ideology. When he came to write *Mein Kampf*, Hitler could assert with chilling confidence that "The basic ideals of the National Socialist Movement are populist (völkisch) and the populist (völkisch) ideas are National-Socialist."

Crucial in asserting the aggressively pure identity of young German and Austrian males, the fencing fraternities had inevitably excluded Jews. So too had the sports clubs, potentially more accessible to the young Karl Rahm. Perhaps the members of these organisations feared that the Jews might excel in athletics as they had in law, medicine, banking and the arts.

I discovered that Jews reacted to exclusion from the sports clubs of Vienna by establishing their own organisations. At the same time they were responding to the call from the late Dr Max Nordau for *muskuljuden*, a term coined by this highly influential eugenicist and Zionist author of *Degeneration* with the precise aim of transforming the image of the Jew. In 1909 Hakoah (Hebrew for strength), the famous Jewish sports club was founded in Vienna.

It was also the city's first Zionist club. Its official programme states: "The Association aims at the physical education of the Jewish people and the raising of its national consciousness. This purpose is to be attained by the cultivation of all branches of physical sport and by the institution of lectures, educational courses, literary, musical and vocal exercises, etc." Hakoah achieved its greatest successes on the football pitch. Their English trainer, Willie Hunter, a former Millwall and Bolton Wanderers player, inspired them to become the first 'enemy' team to resume relations with English sportsmen. In May 1923 the West Ham United team visited Vienna and played against Hakoah in front of a crowd of 65,000 spectators.

Ahead of a return match, Lorenz Bunt, a Hakoah committe member, visited London and, speaking to *The Jewish Chronicle* in August 1923, said: "Despite the tremendous anti-Semitism prevailing in Vienna our young men played Sunday after Sunday in the open fields with the *Magen David* on their breasts, and we gradually won a foremost place among the football teams of the country."

Famously, on Monday 3 September 1923, a Hakoah team of *muskuljuden* beat West Ham United 5–0 at Upton Park.

During its early years the Hakoah club had been short of funds. As I looked into its solution to this problem, I came upon a remarkable man, the club's extraordinarily resourceful honorary president and co-founder. Born in Bohemia on 24 June 1883, Dr Fritz Beda-Löhner (originally Bedrich Loewy, pen name 'Beda') had been brought up and educated in Vienna where he graduated in Law. By the time he was 17, he was showing conspicuous literary talent and began to publish witty, satirical poems.

The new medium of radio quickly made his name. He wrote the lyrics for many operettas including Franz Léhar's *Land of Smiles* in which Richard Tauber became a popular star. A passionate Zionist, Beda had no time for converts believing that those who gave up their Jewish identity did so for materialist reasons. Nor did he believe in assimilation. He believed passionately in justice. When Josephine Baker arrived in Vienna in 1927, the city greeted her as the black devil, the bells of St Paul's sounded the alarm. Beda responded with a pointed lyric in her defence observing wittily that when she shimmied, the whole of Viennese art trembled. His version, *Ausgerechnet Bananen* of 'Yes, we have no bananas', is an equally witty reinterpretation of that song.

In support of Hakoah, Beda organised highly successful concerts which went a long way to securing the club's finances.

On 13 March 1938, the day after the *Anschluss*, Beda was arrested and deported to Dachau. From there he was taken to Buchenwald and then to

Swimming medals belonging to Annemarie Pisker, born 1919, Vienna, now living in London, a member of the Hakoah-Vienna Sports Club and a 1930s Austrian National Champion freestyle swimmer. Swimming medals shown with two medals awarded to her father in the First World War.

Auschwitz where he was murdered in 1942. His wife and two daughters were also killed. Beda had hoped that Franz Léhar would intercede on his behalf since Hitler loved Léhar's music. But Léhar's first concern was that the Führer overlook the race of his Jewish wife. This concern caused him to neglect his friend and colleague.

These facts have contributed to *Dies Irae*, my sequence of connected, speculative poems about Karl Rahm.

Inevitably perhaps, having looked into the life of this Nazi, I wanted to speak to just one more Terezín survivor.

By chance, shopping one day in Cambridge, I met Eva Clarke and later, her mother Anka Bergman who had spent three years in Terezín. Eva reminded me that it was her mother's cousin, Hana Volavková, author and post-war Director of the Prague Jewish Museum, who had arranged for the names of all of the Czech victims to be inscribed on the walls of the city's Pinkas Synagogue. Quite unexpectedly, I had the chance to end the project in Cambridge where it had begun. As an acculturated Jew, Anka had enjoyed a broad education, which had allowed her to become junior backstroke champion.

Anka and her husband, Bernd Nathan, were deported to Terezín on successive transports in December 1941. In February 1944, Anka gave birth to a son, Jiří (Dan) Nathan. The artist Bedrich Fritta gave Anka the pram that had been used by his little son, Tommy. Very sadly, Jiří died two months later of pneumonia.

On 3 September, 1944, Bernd was deported to Auschwitz. Not knowing where he had been sent, Anka volunteered to follow him the next day. She never saw him again but heard from an eye-witness that he had been shot dead in Auschwitz on 18 January 1945.

Pregnant with her daughter, Eva, Anka spent ten days in Auschwitz before being sent to Freiberg Slave Labour Camp in Saxony, ten miles from Dresden. She was there for six months until April 1945 when the camp was evacuated and all the prisoners, about 2,000 women, were loaded onto a train consisting of coal trucks open to the skies. They had no idea where they were going. Anka told me that she was on the train for three weeks with no food and minimal water. Her life was saved by a farmer who, shocked by the sight of a skeletal, pregnant woman, offered her a glass of milk. A Nazi guard raised his whip to strike Anka – and then, unaccountably, he lowered it, allowing her to drink.

Anka went into labour on the coal truck. She struggled onto a cart where she was surrounded by people with typhus and typhoid. But her daughter Eva arrived safely in Mauthausen on 29 April 1945. Two events saved them. On 28 April the Germans had blown up the gas chamber as they were trying to hide incriminating evidence and a few days after Eva's birth the Americans liberated the camp. When eventually they reached Prague, they found one surviving cousin, Olga. Anka asked to stay with her for a few days which became three years.

Our conversations and e-mails prompted the series of poems entitled 'Koblihy' (Doughnuts). Anka was particularly delighted with Beda's version of 'Yes, we have no bananas', a song which she knew well but had not thought about for many years. And, as she held a copy of the music which I had brought, she told me that after the War she had heard a rather aged Richard Tauber sing in *The Land of Smiles*.

When Marion and I began *Faces in the Void*, we had no idea that a Torah scroll exiled from a small Czech town would lead us to so many extraordinary people. The preparation for each exhibition and each presentation we have given has prompted new research, bringing with it a deepening sense of the varied and complex nature of both Jewish identity and the dramatically changing relationship of Jews with local populations.

Following the anti-Semitic riots of 1920 in Prague, Kafka himself wrote to journalist Milena Jesenská:

I've spent all afternoon in the streets, wallowing in the Jew-
baiting. "Prasive plemeno" – "filthy rabble" I heard someone call
the Jews the other day. Isn't it the natural thing to leave the place
where one is hated so much? (For this, Zionism or national feeling
is not needed.) The heroism which consists of staying on in spite
of it all is that of cockroaches which also can't be exterminated
from the bathroom.

His despair contrasts forcefully with the unquenchable optimism of Alice
Sommer-Herz or Anka Bergman imprisoned in Terezín. Anka still protests,
baffled by the paradox: "We were German. My husband was German. But they
took us because we were also Jews."

Throughout our discussions of Czech Jewish identity, Marion and I have drawn on the expertise of a Czech friend, Petr Brod, Head of the Prague Office of the BBC. When we first arrived in Prague he took us to all of the city's Jewish places. Over the years, he has tirelessly introduced us to informative people, to books and articles. A few weeks ago, I e-mailed him about Jewish life under the Soviets. With typical thoughtfulness, he scanned me a letter from the Václav Kopecky collection in the National Archives. It clearly demonstrates the reality of Soviet anti-Semitism: the risk of being labelled Jewish, the continuing existence of racial prejudice. But more striking is the enormous courage of the author, Karel Kreibich. In December 1952, he wrote this letter to his fellow members of the Communist Party Secretariat, questioning their handling of the Slansky trial and asking trenchantly: "Does being of 'Jewish origin' constitute possessing a criminal nature?"

Marion and I have witnessed stories of Jews criminalised and demonised. We have also witnessed the courage of those who succeeded in rescuing them. We have sat in awe listening to stories of endurance from those who survived the effects of Nazi prejudice: extreme cold, starvation, filth, illness and the constant fear of torture, bereavement and death.

As we discussed each contributor's experience of the past, we talked about the transmission of the Holocaust by historians. In his deeply thoughtful book, *Constructing the Holocaust*, published in 2003, Dan Stone writes (p. 54) "In essence, the western tradition of historiography continued unexamined because it too repressed Nazism. Indeed, this can be said to be the basis of tradition; as Michel de Certeau writes in his discussion of Freud, a tradition 'is defined by what it silences', and 'organizes itself as repression.'… In fact, from the 1960s onwards, historians' interests developed and moved towards new areas of study: the voiceless in history, minorities, women, popular culture. When dealing with the Holocaust, however, traditionalist paradigms reigned supreme."

By contrast, in photography and in poetry, Marion and I have attempted to communicate the impact of unique, previously unheard stories. For me, the most extraordinary moment in each meeting has occurred when a survivor has said quite suddenly and always with great generosity, "I've never told anyone else about this …" Invariably, a clearly remembered detail or episode has brought the past sharply to life and become, for both Marion and me, a source of real inspiration.

Religious Jews, acculturated Jews, Zionists, patrilineal Jews and those who supported them – each has a voice as individual as his or her image. The vision of a thousand-year Reich and the industrialised extermination of those

(Opposite) Olga Šronková Anka's only surviving cousin, in her flat in Prague in the 1950s.

Anka Nathan with her daughter Eva, in Prague, 1945.

Hana Volavková with her son Vojta, taken in Prague in 1942.

(Below) Pinkas Synagogue, Prague. Photo taken with kind permission of The Jewish Museum, Prague.

who failed to meet the exacting criteria for membership make the Holocaust a unique event. Nevertheless, the experiences of those persecuted, because they belonged to a small community, bear comparison with the victimisation of other groups which, everywhere in the world, wish to retain their identity.

Although both our encounters and our research brought us into the closest touch with extreme suffering, these also revealed possibilities for survival and regeneration. And it is this transformative sense that finally resists despair.

(Next two pages) Rail Track Memorial, Bahnhofstrasse, Terezín.

POEMS

JIŘÍ KRAUS
NAR. 29 BŘEZNA 1903 – ZEMŘ. 19 ZÁŘÍ 1942.

ALFRED KLAČER
NAR. 18 ŘIJNA 1897 – ZEMŘ. 8 BŘEZNA 1966.

MARIE KLAČEROVÁ
NAR. 10. LEDNA 1905 – ZEMŘ. 9. ŘIJNA 1970.

BLUE ANGEL

for Ester Krausova

I was his blue angel his blond Venus his scarlet Empress
I mean in the flesh
how I was adored
my ears wore doves and shells and willow leaves of gold
    slipped out of velvet
from spills of indigo tissue
I unwrapped a symphony of scents
each in its own cut glass stoppered bottle
I was his sea of black silk lingerie

my God I cherished him
every hair on his wrists and back
his squat dark torso

for him
I mastered the art of Zwetschkenstrudel Linzertorte Apfelstrudel
and the almost hourly mitzvah of coffee
begun silently just after dawn
I peeled and chopped and simmered and stuffed
Jewish charcuterie

but then this murmuring
a street muttering at us just back from a theatre
Everyone should have a robot
a special Jewish robot
and they closed the door of the theatre in his face
and cut off the phone
he couldn't even smoke a cigarette

and Juli whom I'd known for years
pinching Josef's cheek
held him suddenly away
I'd thought to look and see the whole of his perfection
until she said
so … two pips in an apple
isn't he like Jiří
speaking as if her mouth were full of pins
her lips stitched up
and I was sick

52

(Previous pages) Josef Kraus at the grave of his father, Jiří Kraus, 1903–1942.

6 months pregnant and more sick than at 3
and sleepless as a river
I shook all day

Heydrich's murder 1942
Josef just a year and Jana then unborn
my mischling children
lousing up an Aryan family
muddying the gene pool
entarteten
these
my sweetest fruit
כאישון עיני k'ishon einai

and then the payback in Lidice just 10 miles from Prague
right through a still June night
every single man against the wall of Horák's farm
shot by a team of marksmen
Jews from the spa at Terezín trucked across
to ditch 200 punctured bodies
wives daughters lovers children
all high security risk to the budding Aryan state carted off
a place given over to ash
turned back to earth
and nothing said against it

and in that blazing moment I knew I could have nothing said
against my mischling children
no guns put to their heads
he was out their father
I packed and put a 100 kilometres between myself and mein
        jüdischer Geliebter
I made a new name for myself
back in a safe blonde skin

I left no forwarding address
working a farm becoming ordinary invisible
giving them plums and sugar
playing the gramophone
dancing in my boots

but after I heard he hanged himself
I saw too sharply Josef was Jiří's own

...VII		KLEINER RUDOLF		
OTTILIE	1876	HANA		
HANA	1876	MARKÉTA		
MARKÉTA	1889	KLEPETÁŘ OTTO Mor.		
HUGO	1892	KOHN ALFRED		
ANNA	1922	VALTER		
ROBERT	1925	KOHN BEDŘICH		
...VA IRMA	1883	RŮŽENA		
...ANN ALOIS	1884	KOHN FELIX		
MILADA	1877	ZDENKA		
ZDENKA	1885	KOHN KAREL		
RŮŽENA	1865	OTILIE		
...ANN OTTO	1874	EDITA		
MARIE	1899	KOHNOVÁ BERTA		
SYLVA	1901	KOHNOVÁ JOSEFA		
...ANNOVÁ JANA	1910	KOHNOVÁ KONSTANTINA		
JOSEF	1923	EDITA		
MARIE	1943	KOHNOVÁ EMILIE		
KAREL	1864	KOPPERL FRANTIŠEK		
VĚRA	1894	IRENA	1892	
...ANN OTTO	1897	JARA	1913	
OLGA	1922	KOPPERLOVÁ MARTA	1893	
VOJTĚCH	1923	EVA	1892	
JIŘÍ	1895	KRÁSA VÍTĚZSLAV	1894	
...SKÝ ARNOŠT	1894	MARIE	1892	
BEDŘICH Dr. ING.	1928	JARMILA	1891	
GEROVÁ TEREZIE	1924	KRÁSOVÁ EMILIE	1877	
GUSTAV	1894	KRAUS MAX	1882	
	1890	IRMA	1895	
	1887	LAMPLOVÁ MARIE	1870	
	1913	LAŠOVÁ RŮŽENA	1818	
		LAVECKÝ KAREL	1870	
		...REDER ROBERT		

SKIN

for Eliška Levinská

Late November 1942
matka packing
only the best for the Spa
and I whined I can't go in these shoes
what will people think
I'd seen these boots
ankle length
brown and cream calf
slightly tapered with cream leather laces
I knew they would change my life
they'd cradle and kiss my feet
and I'd have a tribe of friends wherever we were going
I believed באמונה שלמה b'emunah sh'leimah
prosím matka prosím
they're not expensive
not for what they are
sei doch nicht so geizig
prosím matka prosím

and my mother
she hid in a farmer's cart from Nemošice to Pardubice
and brought back these boots from Bata Shoes
with money hidden in an attic
they were three sizes too big
I stood in a river
my father stuffed the toes with paper
I was his Liebling

Blessed art Thou oh Lord our God Who has given me such
    beautiful boots

queuing at the station for the train to Terezín 605 people stared

so they have money to burn
who would have thought it

56

(Previous pages) Eliška Levinská at the Holocaust Monument, Pardubice Jewish cemetery.

I hid behind papa
clinging to his coat
he said
she wanted to look her best
our only one kid

snow mud ash blood
for three years everything clung to them
three years working the gardens
tomatoes cucumbers lettuces and kohlrabi
for just one taste the guard who never stopped smoking
        or chewing
had me stand under the sun until I fainted
and when I came round
hit me
eins zwei drei vier fünf
even the bugs did better

in the Kleiderkammer matka lifted the luggage from the old
who'd brought of course the best of everything they could
which was simply perfect for Winterhilfe in Berlin
for faithful German Hausfrauen

then papa disinfected their ageing crumpled talcumed Jewish skin
        and coiffeured hair with dilute Zyklon B
specific against lice
until one day they picked him for a dose in Oświęcim
straight from the train

after Oświęcim and Belsen
and back to Terezín
leaving then for Pardubice
just matka and myself
out of all of us
out of 22
all she said was
and this was all she said of this until she died
haven't they done well
those boots
they've been a second skin
I knew they'd see you through

FAMILY TREE

for Ladislav Novák

Call me the last Jew
Ladislav ben Ladislav
born Pardubice 1953
father of Aleš
born Pardubice 1978
call on me
this cool September morning
here in my pension
a step or two from Tesco and the city's castle
and the plaque crazed with cobwebs marking the Shul crushed by
    the Soviets
call me
Ladislav ben Hana

look
there she is
now
on the screen
Hana Seinerova
visiting Eretz Yisrael
the land
the land
there in Jerusalem
עין לציון צופיה Ayin leZion tzofi'a
and there in Ashdod for the Seder
that's Milan her brother her recovered twin
and how many children
Eden and Gal and Noa and Iris and Shai
you think at simchas
we have fewer than 500
kehile Seiner

but here in Pardubice
I am the last Jew

Hana tastes the bread of affliction
sharp on her gums and tongue

59

Ladislav Novák in his Penzion, Pardubice.

in 1945
11 years old
she staggered out of Ravensbrück
left right right left left left
right into Bergen Belsen

one of Mengele's broken toys

bitten by the typhus bug
lousy little blood sucker
sneaking out of schmattes barely covering her she screamed out
unstitch them quick unpick the stitches quick
seeing other twins
gypsy twins stitched back to back
vein into vein
liver to liver

stitched into loneliness

 coming to how she wanted her brother
bind me to him
bind me

a woman she'd met in Terezín kept her body going
so they could put her on a bus to Prague
and then to Pardubice
with a pay off of 1000 crowns
but no address to speak of

somewhere in this town she found an uncle
his bright new shicksé wife found soup spoons to be polished until
she could see her crimson lips and tongue
sheets to be smooth as paper
and a front step to be whiter than next door's table linen on a
        Sunday
for discharging such light duties she'd take the child in
the little Jew
until her whining that something or other *hurt*
her head her hands her gut her eyes
at times even her heart

– at 14 what could she know of heart –
simply forced her to dismiss her
maybe the home for homeless girls could bear her
she wanted a house of peace

at just 19
the year her lost twin brother left for the Promised Land
Hana married
became Pani Novák
it seemed a final solution
(she barely read or wrote)

now call me Ladislav ben Hana
I am the last Jew

each year I go alone to Eretz Yisrael
 leaving my wife and son
– how could they be Jews –
the Law's the Law
take it or leave it
my Adela's no Jew

but once a year in Eretz Yisrael
just for a week or two
safe in a Jewish skin
I savour a Jewish tongue

could I want more
for me *day – dayenu*

DAMALS

1. That was then

only now that you mention it
she Boýena Kučcová has time at her creased white fingertips
leafing back through 80 years until she was simply 20
standing in this same place
but in a street full of Jews
then their schoolhouse stood where her house stands
next to the rabbi's
and do you know how well they all got on
talking under the bus shelter
under a catholic cross
and do you know
she simply didn't believe how soundlessly they could disappear
in one night
herded to the train to Terezín
and how there's just the one wooden house still standing
standing still

2. Heřmanův Městec

outside beside the mikveh
the sun catches my eyes closing against the flood of light
against a cup a brush a china shard
lifted after 450 years
but left as if a woman say last erev Shabbat
had forgotten them
had moved out of time
had lingered under water flowing over her head
stroking each cropped hair her eyelids forehead breasts
thighs and the inner recesses of her ears
until she was deaf and blind to the world outside her head

the salt tang of leather and smoked fish and a knot of seven
        daughters and sons under her skirts
and her man talking with other men each loudly blessing their God

63

Boýena Kučcová, Drevíkov.

that He had not made them women
but she was nothing but this drowning dreaming moment
    that had nothing to do with purity
with her readiness to receive and nurture life
but which granted her miraculously
a moment's solitude
a real blessing

Mikveh, Heřmanův Městec

3. The deserted synagogue

inside this Shul built in the latest Roman style
arches and fluted columns
blue gold stars and flowers
I imagine 1870
the Germans (at last called Jews)
choosing this architecture in certainty
loving their neighbours' art
though saying finally the spire could go
if their friend the Count would lay the first stone in welcome
and afterwards share their fish
(who would want to dwarf St Batomolij church standing on the square)

I wonder
seeing such gilded beauty
did the Roman Catholic priests smile and ask
were they building heaven on earth
a new Jerusalem
seeing how far these shoemakers thought they'd come
crossing how many rivers seas
out of the wilderness
into this town
and might each adorable stone each blessed lick of paint
each square of blissfully blue glass
speak of a glorious God in the world to come

standing in the gallery built for women
I cannot imagine a simcha
cannot imagine eyes meeting eyes
hands brushing hands
straightening a scarf
smoothing a skirt
or a child's wild curls
hushing her
you can't hear Irma hoping the potato soup will stay hot till
        Shabbat is out
or Marta Helena Zdenka Hermina Rudolfina Bedriska and Anna
asking who's matched with whom
occasionally blessing God

there is not a single voice
not a single breath or thumbprint
not a tallit or kippah
not a single book
there is nothing … nothing

only a lavish emptiness
without consolation
an architecture in loneliness

only here and now Elul 5767 four of us stand and talk in a corridor
and then on a street outside the gate
Eliška born Vienna 1930

daughter of Herta and of Erwin Weiss
    who never came back from Auschwitz
Terézia born in Pardubice 1983 grand-daughter of Eliška
Marion born in London
and myself Jane also born in London

Eliška says

this Rosh Hashanah I will light my candles
that's all that I can do
now there is no community outside Prague

but the four of us talk the New Year
talk honey cake and apples
talk apples and gingerbread
talk fish and jam
talk Eilat and Tel Aviv
talk Ladislav Mare
the town's last Jew who died last Spring

and four Jews four women (making less than half a minyan)
swap more than four languages
and are suddenly more than enough

and Terézia laughing behind her smart new shades gives each of us
a glass of spring water

saying

l'chaim l'chaim
next year in Pardubice
and then
back here again

Synagogue interior, Heřmanův Městec.

Jiří Schreiber sitting in the Memorial Hall, Pardubice Jewish cemetery.

Deportation Record for Jiří Schreiber.

(Previous pages) Bohušovice Station from which prisoners originally had to walk
three kilometres to Terezín. A railway branch line was built by the prisoners
and from June 1943 deportees went directly to the Ghetto.

THE PIOUS PLACE
BY THE RIVER OHŘE
for Jiří Schreiber

this morning Jiří called from Pardubice
said
I've been 80 years in the system
this thing called life
this body wearing thin
a scroll unravelling

but I wanted to tell you about turning 13
1938
that last August in the mountains
after the bar Mitzvah
savouring Czech I made this other pact
on my honour I promise to do my best
to serve the highest Truth and Love at all times faithfully
to fulfil my duties and observe Scout laws
to help my country and my neighbours with my body and my soul

and I dreamed of Tomáš Garrigue Masaryk our President who
     gave our Austrian self a shove

that was my last free summer
spent in the mountains among pines and swirling water
but that boy sleeps in my heart
along with Vilém Singer who didn't make it back

for then the invitation came
to Theresienstadt or Terezín
a spa upstream from Prague for fragile Jews and others who need
     time out
offering special treatment
100 kilos worth of luggage will be more than enough to last
pianos candlesticks skis and porcelain
these will be taken care of
everything is there

even salmon fishing
you will be free to pray
even to play your violins – and sing
Beethoven Bach Mozart Brahms
to talk of course and mail your friends
take tea and coffee cake
and for a treat sardines

1942 and I was 17
they packed us tight as dried fruit in a train crawling to Bohušovice
we hauled the luggage 3 kilometres to Terezín
the Jewish gateway to the East
to Sobibór Birkenau Treblinka Bełżec Oświęcim

the cases ripped the skin from both my hands
I was stripped and sluiced
my father struggled to pretend his naked flesh was just another suit

after two days bed bugs fleas mosquitoes moths rats ran the two square
    meters of this scant world I a Jew was wasting
I was an ass or ox pulling wagons heaped with sewing machines
that no one ever used
once I paused for breath
was hit here on the chin
once for each syllable
Sei nicht böse lach mal

and all that summer they stacked us to the roof
you breathed your own sour breath

September 1942
131 people died each day of jaundice typhoid suicide and TB
the guards nodded smiled and said Die Uhr tickt gut
winter eats the old
then hissed
there is this regrettable backlog of bodies disfiguring our model
    Ghetto
in the interests of hygienic correctness
you will implement these orders of …
כשרות Kashrut

(Arbeit macht frei)
load the coffins pull the carts
work the crematorium
so … you will burn your dead
komm you bake bread
you've even roasted meat
you know to treat these ovens with respect
kerosene provides an even heat
an everlasting flame
but a body keeps its pockets of resistance
protein retards the process of reduction
let the fire fall
you'll have charred flesh
let it flare
bone fuses to the steel
this you'll have to clean with your bare skin
but you'll get the feel
you know your Volksmaterial so well
Wissenschaft des Judentums
and by the way
wombs kindle well
even dead girls are fierier than men

in the interest of optimum performance
and high turnover
90 must go each day

each body went to ash in forty minutes
(let's say forty years)
to be panned like river sand for a Punkt of gold melted from just
        one tooth

we put the ash in boxes
each with a name and number pasted on
thirty thousand kept in a Columbarium named for the keeping of doves
see the niches
waiting for carved stone urns
but we were not worthy of urns
we were
– smell this –

sulphur copper burned liver tanned leather shit
sent up in smoke

November '44
most of the men sent East
SS officers wanted modern working conditions and comfortable
    leisure facilities

ordered the remnant left behind – all women – to build a cinema a
    kitchen and a bright new dining room

Theresienstadt must keep its place as best kept Ghetto
echo the chorus of approval from the impeccable Red Cross
round on round of applause for outstanding cultural and leisure
    facilities religious and medical care

now why not give the Yid kids and the frail a chance to feel truly
    special
those left in the cold playing a vital role

let those poxy boxes go

(Arbeit macht frei)
a few nights' work

imagine in the icy darkness
a double line of Jewish hands
hour after hour
passing thirty thousand boxes of their dead
cramming them into trucks
– small crates of vegetables –

imagine now a box split open
putting into your hands a chip of bone
a pinch of ash
how do you brush this off

imagine a patch of smoky light
catching your name on a box
and you can't just pass it on

but there's a guard up against you needling
(Arbeit macht frei)
remember you'll be paid in extra sugar
and your starved mouth drools
but you have dipped your fingers in your mother's ash
– never mind a ration of grey sugar –
what on earth now can you taste or touch
what bracha say

in this impossible place twenty choice young men emptied the boxes in
      an endless soundless fall
coating the water
leaving scum
and then under black light burned them

in case they still held anything they might pass on
say blood on scrubbed and polished German hands
they were taken out and shot against a wall in the Small Fortress
seeing the bullets come

(Arbeit macht frei)

this is the place of piety named for duty and obligation
this is a river in memory
נהר השמות n'har hashemot
shed light on this water
on layers of salts and ash

I am scattering the water with these crumbs
these crumbs of my forgetfulness

נזכור שארית נחלתנו nizkor sh'erit nakhalatenu

(Next two pages) The Pious Place Memorial, Terezín.

75

TWO POEMS FOR ALICE SOMMER-HERZ

GEDENKSTÄTTE

this is a river of memory
Die Eger
named in German for the craft of the salmon
storing the thousand differing scents of home
siblings gravel weed oak leaves and murder in the dust of human
     skin picked up before the voyage out at 6 months old
ready for a 300 miles swim to the North Sea
salt on her soft lip
a year or maybe five spent cutting her teeth making waves
going a bit blue the weeks before the long haul back
the touch of scent after scent
telling her *stay still or go against the flow*
she must keep going before that final fling
that flight into dry air and charging water
before the swim back home
     to Fichtelgebirge
the tang of stone and fir trees
the time and place to spawn

named in Czech for a molten underworld
this is teka Ohře
putting warmth against the trace of murder
calling water balm
today t-shirt weather heats the skin
even if the wind tugs the willows troubles the oaks
and coming up against a sudden lump of quartz the water kicks
     itself
but this is no real bother
this slight flurry lifting sand gravel clay a salmon's tooth a pinch of ash

upstream in 1812 at Karlsbad Beethoven sipped the river's
     minerals
longing to soothe his searing gut
he took a hot tub
and felt her hands stroking forehead cheek-bones nape shoulders
     vertebrae one by one

with just her fingertips and hair
his *Unsterbliche Geliebte*
his adorable immortal beloved
he imagined her practising scales
his lips touched her ears and tasted salt
she at the tip of his tongue
dolcemente subito
leicht bewegt
and so he caught her every breath her every heart beat under him
the devil could take Goethe and his sniping
Ludwig must you be so wild
can't you comb your hair
you never know what Prince might be looking
Johann would have sold his soul for the hint of a Kaiser's smile
the cafés brimmed with his fans
but Ludwig he could hear
within his flawless inner ear
yes he could hear his eighth unfolding out of her hands which were
becoming his
his sweet salt girl
but then she left him
he at 42
she fled
there were no more letters
his ears drummed *einsam einsam einsam*
and whirred and shrilled
felt filled with silt
yet flooded with grief he dreamed her dancing a Haydn minuet *gracioso*
like old times
waking he stamped his foot *sforzando*
he would not drown in grief
he ordered the sharpest quill
he'd make the bar lines disappear
music for 1812
a pulsing symphony the sound of irony
and each phrase stemmed the tide of history
and loneliness and loss

(Next two pages) Alice Sommer-Herz, listening to Jane reading
her poem 'Appassionata' for the first time, London, 2008.

79

APPASSIONATA

1

So why should I die
at 104 why should I go gently
or furiously
at midnight or between the hours of two and four a.m.
or later the same day
or any day soon
today I don't have time
I am far from ghostly
I'm remembering Franz
Kafka to you of course
such loud brown eyes
and a mouth at the edge of a smile

picture myself and Marianne
at seven
walking him into the forest
some July afternoon
too warm for socks or sleeves
our slight fingers locked in his
making for the blue green cool of pines
and a log to perch on
and then he
squat on a stone
took us out of story into story
where he took a late night ride on the shoulders of a stranger
and told us
listen
laugh more softly
there's a beetle sleeping under the leaf mould
you wouldn't want to wake

and he ran Marianne's shuddering finger tip over its hard skin
said
see how its eyes catch the light
it is as if each lens takes in a different bit of leaf
and melds the pieces

before it can take a bite
don't polish it off

so
while I remember the rise and fall of his voice
though I know he didn't know what to do with himself
outside the story
if he could kiss Dora
and not take her to the Chuppah
(his skin was not so hard)
considering all this
why should I die

2

So
October 1944
the day they sent my husband East
and the same day I had to tell my son of 7
there was nothing more to eat
but would he please not chew the mattress
imagine 4.00 a.m.
imagine his lips blue against his pink tongue
imagine leaving him
my Brundibár sparrow
to scrub linen and my hands
imagine him saying into the mattress
into the dark
Tonight I'll be alone
I know you'll follow papa
I put a finger to his lips
and promised him a gift
a nice surprise

that day Ludwig raged inside my head
putting my fingers to his latest longest keyboard
opening arpeggio on arpeggio
on the monstrous silence of a friend
another person not to talk to
believe me

I saw him walking the Vienna woods
the sunlight lavish on rocks and pines and streams

and still I heard him howl

and then quite suddenly compose himself
note after touchy note
sonata apasionata
I heard him growl
this is no music for cowards

and you know
when I walked into the room after 16 hours washing clothes
my son stood absolutely still
and his face was
should I say
illuminated
and I said *tonight I will play for you*
Beethoven
piano e pianissimo

and you will see

there is
      no time
          to die

(Previous two pages) Alice Sommer-Herz
with pictures of her son, cellist Ralph Sommer.

86

Alice playing the piano, London, 2006.

I SPEAK TO THE CHILD
THAT I WAS

for Sir Nicholas Winton and Vera Gissing

1

3rd September 1939 my sister and I wait in England for our two
    cousins
savouring already Czech bread and words
Honza and Tommy wait for their train to pull out of the station
out of Prague and Germany out of their lives
Aunt Marti and Uncle Gustav wait on the platform at midnight
if we've forgotten anything we'll send it on
write as soon as you arrive
of course they'll like you
what's not to like

no one says goodbye

it can't be long now
surely
there's someone coming he's bound to know

raus raus raus
alles aus
in Ordnung
Heil Hitler

the last train's been and gone
this one's out of order
raus raus raus

catching fear from adult eyes 250 children go quiet as stone

days years lives later teenagers in Auschwitz
Honza and Tommy were less than cockroaches

up against the wire they met each train packed with matted hair
    and skinny limbs

era Gissing in her garden.

they called their family's names
when Aunt Marti staggered through the gate
she heard her own
and scanned a line of faces mouths eyes stretched skin and bone
liebe Gott none of those crazed skulls is mine
Baruch ha Shem
and her boys saw some white haired stranger wearing their
      mother's clothes

this comes to me just like that
I can be sitting still
or talking as I am today to you
or stooping to adjust a pinching shoe
or dreaming in the garden

and touching a rose that creeps along the fence
I see them
those four
caught in that moment
passing each other by

Honzi and Thomas
Marti their mother
and my Diamond mother Irma

thinking of them I've brought white roses in
and some for Nicky the friend who got me out
a planet on his own

2

Nicky says
appeasement really is a dirty word
I can't forget how Chamberlain betrayed those far away people
Czechs Slovaks Moravians and Bohemians
saying in 1938
I am a man of peace
who cannot go to war for so small a nation
I can't forget that letter to his sister after Kristallnacht
Jews aren't a lovable people

I don't care for them myself
but that can't be enough to cause a Pogrom
and so I went to war for Jewish children
instead of ski-ing

years later I had this friend
nice chap but oh he hated Jews
a bit of a Neville Chamberlain himself
now what I want to know what I keep on asking
is
how can you tell a Czech how can you know a Jew

I invited 60 Jewish friends down here to a party
and that one non-Jew that ordinary decent man
and when he called to thank me for such a bright evening
such fine wine and fish and lemon syllabub
and finer conversation
almost blowing kisses down the mouthpiece
he murmured
I know that I can speak my heart to you
such a joy you asked no flagrant flaunting high pitched little Jew
Nicholas I always knew that I could absolutely count on you
you're one of the truly few
George I said
I have some news for you
something you'll need to chew on and to digest
last night more than sixty Jews danced here in my place
we get everywhere
my dear
at last night's little supper
you were the only Gentile here

but no one stared and so far no one's said a single unkind word

91

(Next two pages) Sir Nicholas Winton in his home.

THREE POEMS FOR WINIFRED NEW

POLITIK 1

In the end my mother said
all right I can see you're both dreaming of the dance floor
I suppose I'll take you
myself or your brother
don't think you're going out alone

well there were so many airmen
waiting near the door
and none of them local

and after a bit I thought
as well him as another
as well him
after all for 3 weeks running
he'd held open the door to let me in

it wasn't only how he'd come from Czechosloavkia
late December 1939
just after Dunkirk
he and another Josef
come to join the RAF
it wasn't only fire in his eyes
the look of *we won't be done for*
or the laughter when we danced
ever tried the slow waltz
when you're folded up with laughter

but that accent of his
what he made of English
and his promise of a life lived on his farm
the Horák farm at Lidice near Prague
tobogganing each winter mile on mile
a summer crop of dark skinned plums
 to turn to slivovice against the cold

and I imagined them

96

(Václav and Josef)
(Michael and Paul)
Czech tongued sons still at home in English

when we married at Brize Norton my sweet minded mother said
no babies now
not till this War is ended
just remember
but never said how I was going to stop them
Václav came September '42
and little Joe for Christmas '43

as soon as that War ended home we went
into our new Czech life
the boys just 3 and 2

who could take Lidice in
a burned out empty place stretching miles
a single wooden cross
and a few stones from his farm
15 of the Horák family gone
Joe's sister haunted by her murdered baby
squealing with laughter at each feeding time
as if she were alive
calling me *that dreaded English woman*
and all those other women thin and huddled
buried inside themselves
their eyes darting

in February '48 the Soviets put
a blood red full stop to what life we had
bloody Soviets
but they'd come to stay
the neighbours shouted
you work for the state
get out and work today
Sunday's just the same as any other day

as if I didn't have the boys
Peppi and Ku
Pepper and Salt

because of me Josef lost his work
he was so quiet about it
simply said

Siberia's really no place for the boys
so let's toboggan out
Austria's just next door
I thought
how the hell d'you brake at break neck speed
a child sat on your lap
snow whipped up and stinging
and trees lumbering towards you
they blundered into my dreams
and seized the children by the hair

we were going to leave from a hostel on the border
only the boys caught measles

Tuesday 6 April 1948 I was 24
our sons and I flew back to our English home
and at the airport the Soviets seized my birthday gift from Joe
a bracelet made of gold

he walked to Vienna on his own
and came back here

he never should have died my test pilot my Joe
he came out of his plane alive
crash landing in black weather
January 18 1949

and some kind farmer moved him out of the wet
he meant it for the best

but Josef bled to death

Josef Horák with a photograph of his father, Pilot Officer Josef Horák .

Single Wooden Cross, Lidice, c.1945.

POLITIK 2

Out of all those 106 Lidice children who stood as if accused
    of plotting Heydrich's murder
I dream of two
not that I knew my niece Venceslava Kohlicková
and Anitshka her own mother hardly had the time
after she'd laboured utterly alone
gripping her own hands
so an SS face wouldn't blight the threshold of
    her new baby's world

the night the Germans came they had to keep
    their men in line and on their toes
if a target shook a German nerve
that target had to go
at 9 months gone Anitshka was
    just such a moving target
and so she was forced to leave
simply so a German could save face
along with family and closest friends

Václav they'd shot in Prague which was more convenient
and admirably suited to the purpose

for 14 days Anitschka wouldn't leave her baby
not for a scant second
 until they took her down for questioning
just for an hour just to clarify some details
nothing too problematic they said
we'll take care of your little one

three years later out of the camp at Ravensbrück
she and Václav's mother kept death waiting
said *No not here not now*
and stumbled home
they found their village wasn't so much as rubble
only a field of swaying rye
 and no cry left them

POLITIK 3

I can't remember his name
 nor exactly when he came
but I can see his mother standing staring at him
as if she were dreaming him
and the woman gently pushing the boy towards her
the woman who had brought him back from the dead

she said his name over and over
as if she were trying to make it stick
it seemed lost on him
and now it's gone from me

he didn't take long to get his tongue round Czech
– you must remember him –
he used to come to play
he'd build a heap of stones to knock down one by one
and give each one a German name
which you would say in Czech and he would copy
at Christmas time they put him on TV
their little puppet
he only mouthed the English
while someone spoke the unknown words behind him

he always called his mother mutti
until one day she looked at him and said
I thought you'd be the son I lost come back from Ravensbrück
they said you looked like me

he said
I didn't want to come
but no one asked me

and one day shortly after they took him away in a van
it must have been rough going
all the way back to Germany
words for liebling streaming through his mind
drahoušek miláček mazlíček

what ever was his name
what **did** we call that boy

THREE POEMS FOR MARTIN GLAS

GAN EDEN

after they closed the parks and gardens all over Prague
the city went grey overnight
cobbles asphalte mud stretched under your feet
giving you concrete fever
April 1942 the Germans shoved us on the train to Terezín
this was my Hell and Paradise
once prone on the battlements I lay in gan Eden
one afternoon different from all others
grass stroked my heels and cheeks and fingertips
and somewhere on a wall inside the Ghetto
a single blackbird lifted up her head
and gave me note after glowing note

RATION

late Summer 1940 the cafés and the restaurants
where for years we'd sipped whipped cream
on apple cake and coffee
and had talked the politics of art
and of course the art of politics
closed
only to us
mutti said
so we take coffee at home
where's the difference
who can't make apple cake and strudel

in January we couldn't
apples were forbidden fruit
only to us
mutti used jars of pears and plums

in June
there was no more sugar
only for us

(Previous pages) Martin Glas.

Ramparts, Terezín.

mutti said
so we have honey
aren't we blessed

so then they said
beans
as if Jews need beans
so lentils butter beans black eyed beans
were taken
only from us
mutti said
Baruch ha Shem
we still have cabbages

in October 1941 they said
as if Jews need jam or marmalade
so they took these too
only from us

105

(Next two pages) Map of Terezín, annotated by Martin Glas' father,
who gave it to him on their arrival in the Ghetto.

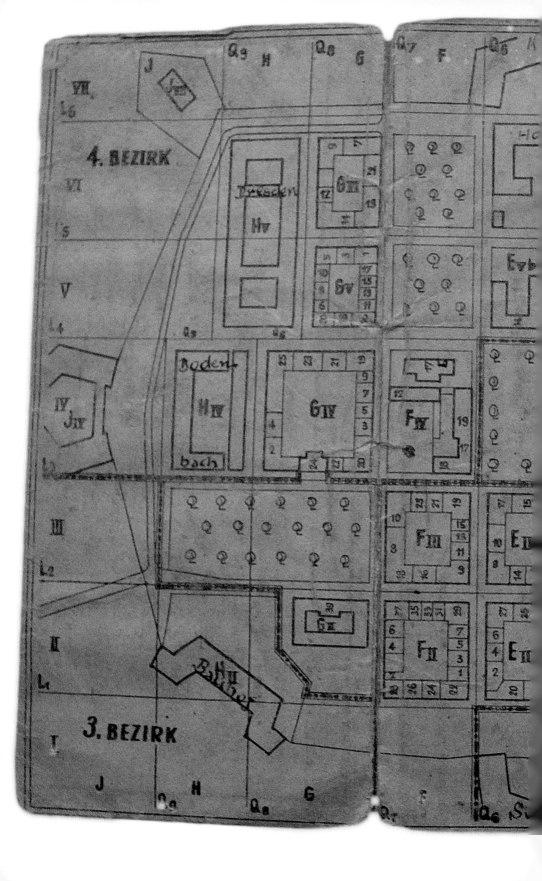

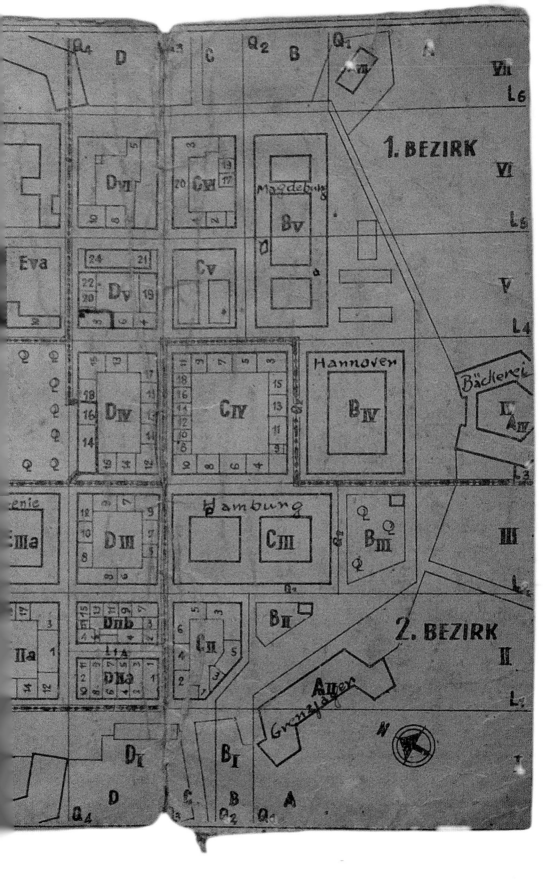

cheese went next
then fish and chicken and venison
taken
only from us
and still mutti said
we still have eggs
and smiled

November came
that month they said
as if Jews need onions
taking them
only from us
and only then did mutti start to cry

TOMATOPHOBIA

In Terezín my mother grew stupice tomatoes
tolerant of frost torrential rain and sharpening sun
in August she fed me fifty every day
certain of their goodness
today I cannot touch one green or red
but then we traded them for grains of sugar
or a square of bread
 and a once in that lifetime miraculous promise of marmalade
a single spoonful put straight in my mouth
left my tongue stung and wanting
and tepid Wassersuppe waiting

at 7.20 pünktlich we played count the fleas in ears on eyelids
and caught behind our knees
this was our new sport
not that I beat the score of twenty-eight
I was always too small to be sporty
Auschwitz would have done for me

they said in Terezín,
you could stay the mensch you'd always been
and when I was sick
jaundiced in hospital

I watched an eighty year old woman kiss
        her five year grandson head to toe
knowing she would go East
today I'm sure that meant far more to him
than all the stories we produced in Domov
the name I chose to call our paper
meaning heim or home

and home was made of words

my father drew a map to keep me going
so you won't ever lose yourself in here
after my father went to Oświęcim
in the last of all compartments
on the last of all those transports chosen to go out
after we staggered back to Prague
and heard that he'd been gassed
I thought the synagogue would take me in
I was just 14
instead the rabbi said
a real Jew would know you aren't a Jew within the Law
your mother was a gentile
you can't be one of us
convert and then we'll see if might welcome you

again my father went to dust
my father Julian Glas
as if we hadn't been in Terezín
as if we'd played some game
and as the rabbi spoke God fled before the faces
        of my 20 loved and dead

I turned and walked away

it's good we're talking here today
even in this annex of the Shul
where they let me come to meet with you

you know that I'm a Jew

109

(Next two pages) Jägergasse, Terezín.

FAMILY

Jerusalem 16 Tevet 5768
25 December 2007
Fourth Day of Chanukah

1 Letter to Miri
for Miriam Loukotová

Shalom Miri

here in Jerusalem on the corner of King George Avenue and Ben Yehuda
    Street
a rabbi lit possibly the world's tallest chanukiah
electrifying the city

I wandered through the Old City savouring sesame rolls
and histories stitched by women
dreaming of a wedding
murmuring of empty marriages
asking how to charm a husband stubborn as a camel
carpets gowns cushions glowing with vines and cypress trees and sacred
    birds
are brought to door after door
quickened by expert fingers
turned in front of my face
by husbands brothers fathers sons
open to offers
seeing tomorrow is Al Hijreya
marking another trip from darkness into life
after the prophet's move from Mecca to Medina
we can discuss the price of changing the world of
    Nablus Hebron Gaza Galilee and Ramallah
in light of the festival

in light of Chanukah I think of you
of Ron and Eli lighting your candles
and saying the blessings
– as if Hebrew were their mother tongue –
at home in Prague where so many scrolls tefillin candlesticks
Kiddush cups

114

(Previous two pages) Vlasta Fošenbauerová.

Tefillin (Phylacteries), worn by Jews during morning prayers, collected in Prague during the German occupation. Photo taken with kind permission of The Jewish Museum, Prague.

Jewish fixtures and fittings
sit still under glass
I imagine a line of kindled lights
reflected in mirrors and windows from chanukiot etched with
almonds fluted flowers stars olive leaves
folded into gold
or silver twists
or plain wood cooled with clay
lit from the right
rippling light scripts the tale of
    Judah Maccabee
and the later eight day miracle of oil
that purged the Temple of a tribe of
    temperamental gods
and then
this small family Midrash
your grandfather František Stern born 1897 walked out of
    Auschwitz
אוד מוצל מאש od mutzal m'eish
the remnant saved from the fire
you said

he couldn't say what happened
couldn't pierce the silent hinterland
his fear I think of not being understood
flowed through my childhood
but when we lit the Shabbat candles
week after week
my grandmother my mother and myself
and the chanukkiah
season after season
(even under the Soviets)
I remember he would stroke my cheek
here where the reflected light touched my skin
and his fingers caught the light

years ago in Slovakia that moment broke the silence
and touches me
at this festival and this season

Thank you Miri
chag sameach

Jane

2 Looking forward
for Eva Loukotová

in January 1945 the Nazis quick marched your mother
        Vlasta Fošenbauerová through the ice and dark
        to the train to Terezín
she'd bundled Pavel her feverish year old son
across to the neighbours
saying *take him to hospital*
now
he must go now
his cry went with her

late in her life she told him how in Terezín
she'd cradled her best friend's child
sometimes at night he'd stirred against her calling for his mother

Eva Loukotová and her family.
Photo taken at the Lauder Gur Aryeh Jewish Community Elementary School, Prague, in September, on the first day of term, when families accompany their children to register for the academic year.

deported East and dead
and turning in her sleep she'd murmured *Pavel Pavel*
and startled into wakefulness
ached for a child she held
and one she couldn't hold

when she walked back home
out of Terezín
she knew that being a Jew was a torn tallit and a waiting son's rage

only much later she found there was just one good thing to that risky legacy
one gift in consolation
a grandson travelling to Jerusalem
and meeting there with Miri
and bringing her here to Prague

The gate leading from the Administration Courtyard to the First Prison Yard and prisoner's cells, Small Fortress, Terezín.

DIES IRAE

1

In the end music didn't save him
ausgerechnet Beda
the little Bohemian Fritz

thinking he'd kept in line
digging stones in Monowice Buna
his fingers slit in the service of I G Farben
keeping Volkswagens in tyres
and Wehrmacht boots well heeled

when I heard I had to laugh
I Karl Rahm
Kommandant of Theresienstadt
I felt curious about his death

did they beat him in time to his endless maddening wheezing
or did they syncopate the blows
in time to his sneezing

118

I heard he'd reported sick
the morning of his death
17 October 1942
that he seemed squeezed of breath
no doubt they thought it part of his old trickery
his 'verbal wizardry'
and sent him off to put in a decent day's work
and then he slowed the whole lot of them
imagine an entire workforce brought to a full stop
by a Jewish slug
no wonder they gave him a kicking
I can't understand why they didn't finish the job
what made them walk away
leaving more men to waste their time
our time
Reich time
holding a dying nothing

Franz kept his wits about him
no special pleading for this little Jew
ausgerechnet Beda
(whose words had made his music sing)

needing Papa Hitler
(Sieg Heil)
to look kindly on him
so he could have and hold
his jüdische Sophie
his *ganzes Herz*
he closed his eyes to Beda
whispering Germania is the only *land of smiles*

2

that little Beda though
he thought he'd made it
years ago in Vienna
smiling kissing wheedling
needling me
he and his unforgettable

119

Ausgerechnet Bananen
ausgerechnet Josephine
ausgerechnet die schwarze Hexe
ein Teufelskind
charming me
disarming me
without my seeing even the least shimmer of her
not a hair of her sleek oiled head
(as if it had slipped through my fingers)
not a shimmy of dark shoulders

what had she to do with me
soft skinned thirteen

suburban
Beda's flash Vienna beyond me

what really got me wasn't the sex
(mostly quick
in the dark and undercover)
purged weekly in confession

do you know what she did
after all the sermons
after all the church bells
rung out in warning
and the original theatre closed against her
she came on like a bride of Christ
a black woman wearing cream silk buttoned up to the chin
meek as meine Mutter

she lulled Vienna

Pretty little baby
I'm in love with you

beautiful marvellous simply adorable

chanted by every Jew on the Ringstraße
as if they were each her *Jüdisches kindchen*

all her little black girls and boys
ausgerechnet Josephine
Empress Josephine
shaking us at the root

3

who was that man on the football pitch in June 1925
almost before my time

Hakoah versus Vienna
it should have been a walkover

the closing moments and that Jew struggles to save a goal
and wrenches his shoulder
hears the muscles tear
so much we thought for Muskul Judentum
brawny Jews
nothing more ridiculous
it's all over
we've drawn
we thought
watching him leave the pitch

glad to see the back of him

but then there he was
minutes later
making a comeback
his arm in a sling
and doing a deal with the striker
smiling and nodding
and the ball is at his feet
and he's onto it
and he Alexander Fabian Jewish goalie eases it into the net

dies irae dies illa

I've waited so long for peace
worked with my hands
turning tools

pursuing exactitude
steel cool
for the sake of a thousand years of certainty
and a heroic German history

4

tomorrow everything's going to work
the schedule's foolproof
last month we sent
seven thousand five hundred *items* out East
the children got the hang of carting luggage to the train
the orphans and the sick went first
(I don't want questions about missing parents)
and it must be said
most consumptive prisoners are as good as dead
I sent Czechs Germans Austrians and Dutch
fair is always fair
and the choosing took some doing
what with the claims to exemption
but I and Judenalteste Eppstein worked as one

we cleared the air and
now we have
Glück und Komfort
SS Obergruppenführer Karl Frank who's cleaning up Bohemia
(what a wonderful job he did in Lidice)
and Quisling Minister Moravec have signalled their approval

I've double-checked each stage along the route
the café laundry workshops and the sports ground
the girls know when to sing
the bakers in white gloves will load the loaves
the band knows when to play
the flower pots are placed with care
no one can say
but look the players' feet are bare
or ask how many Jews have in fact died in here

if any painter dares to show a sketch of sagging shoulders or stone blind
    eyes
I'll pulp his hands

Bare communal cell for Jewish prisoners, Small Fortress, Terezín.

let me sit down taste wine and have a smoke
though *ausgerechnet Josephine*
ausgerechnet Fabian
ausgerechnet Verdi
(dies irae dies illa)
threaten my moment's peace

and could put a man off his stroke

SIX POEMS FOR ANKA BERGMAN

1 Tea Time

when the German soldiers marched in they didn't look at her
they merely got on with the vital job of breaking after entering
of tearing cushions
of tearing down curtains
of pulling open drawers and slinging letters cards address books journals
      on the floor
of clearing the mantle shelf of photographs and scattering the glass
of tearing open envelopes notebooks folders invitations records

they threw themselves into their work
upturning chairs
slitting upholstery
unstitching her house
and she combed her mind for whatever they were missing
and might hope to find

and all the time she stood still and quiet
until suddenly they wiped their faces on their sleeves
she let them exhale and then once more draw breath
and then she said
so now would you perhaps like tea and something light to eat
and when they nodded almost eagerly like any pack of boys
she quietly righted her chairs
and covered the table with a white embroidered cloth
and lifted down the porcelain cups

and while the water boiled
she tucked a wad of notes inside her blouse

submissive to the laws forbidding sugar to her kind
she offered them jam to sweeten their black tea
talking all the time
mostly about the food they missed
Mozart bonbons gulasch viener schnitzel
until they left wiping their mouths on white napkins
which she'd hemmed

126

(Previous pages) Eva Clarke with her mother Anka Bergman, Cambridge.

as if they were new to Prague
merely a couple of unexpected guests

2 Koblihy

December 1941
Bernd left first
I packed cooking pots and pans and spoons
and a few extra woollen jumpers
in case the heating failed
and then at the last moment
I scooped two dozen koblihy
Pfannkuchen left over from Chanukah into a box
and tied it up with string

these were Bernd's favourites
folk food
sweet and hot for winter
jam packed

we waited three days to leave
sleeping skull against skull
hundreds of us
before the march to the train
tugging bags
red currant jam seeping from the box
soaking the cardboard
and a teenage guard carping

es ist scheiß egal ob die schachtel mit kommt

as if at 24 I were a box about to fall apart
at the first sign of trouble

I tightened the string
and gathered up my suit case my hand bag and my doughnuts

and three days later
in the Dresden Barracks
I gave Bernd his little treat

3 Turnip

fifteen people waited for me daily
sister parents in laws cousins aunts uncles

assigned to distribute food I had to keep them going
sometimes an extra turnip
sometimes half a carrot
sometimes a raw potato
too little to live
too much to die

but please God
enough

but every time I gave my mother a turnip
or a cup of milk
or thicker soup

another light boned woman
peeled of dignity
shit heeled
slipped on the straw
and died

4 Anniversary

15th May 1942
sixteen months after we'd left Prague
two years after he'd married me
more than two thousand dead
some on their feet queuing for the latrines

I thought
perhaps he'll bring salami
perhaps an extra dumpling
perhaps perhaps

and all that day I wondered
waiting for Bernd to come

and when he came
running from barracks to barracks
holding his nose against the reek of death

he held out
in this nowhere place
a single dazzling rose

5 L'Chaim

1 Bereshit 1. 28
Be fertile and increase. Fill the earth ...

Keeping the first mitzvah made you unforgivable
according to the Ghetto regulations
handed down from SS General Eichmann
to Dr Siegfried Seidl
our first ruler

twelve girls shoved into a barracks room
knew sex was normal
necessary
part of the old mundane forbidden world
but in Terezín
miraculous as koblihy dipped in icing sugar
so
when a lover stealing time
crept across
we knew to turn away fake sleep or slip outside

after such snatched love
when the hard watchfulness that kept you going through the day melted
and you and he were each a sweet soft touch to one other
five of us conceived

handing us each a formal piece of paper
a guard asked us to sign
something about handing over our babies after birth
something about *euthanasia*

none of us knew the meaning of the word

2

I gave birth in the hospital

no question of medication
(even for constipation)

February 1944
five Jewish obstetricians helped Jiří into the world
talking me out of pain
with story after story

for two months I walked him in Tommy Fritta's pram
the mountains were shrouded in snow
I fought to keep him from the cutting wind
and gusting builders' rubble

I showed him clusters of violets on newly painted window sills
in our newly named town
now the
Jewish Settlement Area of Theresienstadt
I said
it will be all right
all will be well

but then he gasped for breath
twisting and turning his head for air
his body shuddering

the doctor said
dust in the lungs

maybe because of the Verschönerung

 he has an incurable infection

pneumonia seized him
and when he died the white card box they put him in
looked oh so very small

6 Race

after they sent my husband East
I asked to follow
sure that nothing worse could happen
see you tomorrow I promised
waving him off
a last pouted kiss
and his hand brushing my belly
it was 30th October 1944
the last time that we met

once there without him
time and again I took off my clothes
and ran between two lines of German guards
their steel eyes probing me
at 4.00 a.m or 6.00 in the evening
when it was always black and freezing

each time I told myself
look it's just another swim you're going to win
never mind who's watching
and held my rounding stomach in

once and just the once I met Herr Mengele
Herr Doktor Joseph Mengele
stud among Nazi studs
selections were his thing
he couldn't get enough of choosing Jews to burn
or slowly to dismember

addicted to data collection
he kept a wall of eyes
mostly prised from twins
blue green grey
grey green green blue and violet
each meticulously labelled
but speaking eugenically
meaningless and blind

eye to eye with me he simply said
ausgezeichnetes Material
whistled a snatch of Lohengrin
twirled his cane and turned his face

dissecting my performance coldly later
Anka I said *you ran a flawless race*

Anka Bergman looking at the music of *You Are My Heart's Delight* by Franz Léhar, words by Fritz Löhner-Beda.

The Dresden barracks, a dormitory for women prisoners with the camp's prison in the cellar. Both Eliška Levinská, her mother and Anka Bergman were held here.

Aron Ha'Kodesh (Ark) in the oldest surviving synagogue north of the Alps, built probably in the last third of the thirteenth century. *Altneuschul* (Old New Synagogue), Prague.

Prayer benches and *Bima* (elevated platform) in the oldest surviving synagogue north of the Alps. *Altneuschul* (Old New Synagogue), Prague.

HISTORICAL AFTERWORD

Faces in the Void explores the continuing impact of the Second World War on the lives of Czech Jews. After the First World War, the Austro-Hungarian Empire fell and was replaced in 1918 by the independent republic of Czechoslovakia and several other countries. This new republic included Bohemia, Moravia and Silesia, parts of the Kingdom of Hungary (Slovakia and the Carpathian Ruthenia) and sizeable lands where German, Hungarian, Polish and Ruthenian were the dominant spoken languages. In the wake of the Second World War, the Czech Soviet government came to power in 1946 and ruled until 1989 when the Velvet Revolution began to restore democracy.

The Jewish communities of the present day Czech Republic date back, in some cases, to the end of the ninth century. When Germany occupied Czechoslovakia in March 1939, about a quarter of a million Jews were trapped in Bohemia, Moravia and Slovakia. They were increasingly persecuted and, in 1942, mass transports to the ghetto and concentration camp of Terezín/Theresienstadt began. Built in the late eighteenth century in Bohemia, some 50 kilometres north of Prague, the fortress Terezín, known in German as Theresienstadt, was part of Emperor Joseph II's defence programme. He named it after his mother, Maria Theresa of Austria. In peace time, the fortress housed some 5,000 soldiers but during war it could accommodate 11,000. In September 1942, the Nazis held 58,491 in what had become Ghetto Terezín. As a carefully planned part of their extermination machine, it served both as a labour camp and a transit camp.

Some 144,000 European Jews, the majority of whom were Czech, were sent to Terezín. Of the Jews from elsewhere, most were elderly, and were told they would find a settlement specially adapted to their needs. About 33,000 prisoners, a quarter of the inmates, died in the ghetto, mostly from hunger and disease and from the typhus epidemic which struck at the end of the war. Appalling conditions arising from the high concentration of vulnerable prisoners contributed to the death toll. About 88,000 were deported to Auschwitz and other extermination camps. At the end of the war, there were some 17,000 survivors. Of 15,000 children who had lived in the camp's children's home only 93 survived.

In the summer of 1939, Adolf Eichmann became responsible for planning the expulsion of Czech Jews from the newly annexed Protectorate of Bohemia and Moravia. Having established a model in Vienna, he set up a Central Office

Memorial to the Deportation of the Jews, by Helga Hošková, Prague.

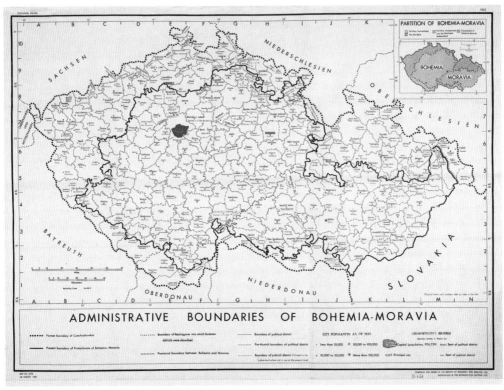

Administrative boundaries of Bohemia Moravia in 1943, showing Prague, Pardubice and
Terezín. With kind permission of Cambridge University Library.

The execution ground, Small Fortress, Terezín.

Coffins in the Mortuary, Terezín.

for Jewish Emigration (Reichszentrale für Jüdische Auswanderung – RSHA) in Prague. In Autumn 1941, Heydrich, Chief of the RSHA IV B 4, asked him to address the Wannsee Conference on the implementation of the Final Solution. Eichmann was therefore a key figure in planning the fate of Czech Jews.

Before the deportations to Terezín began, a Jewish Council of Elders (the Altestenrat) was established in the Prague Jewish Community. Within Terezín, the Altestenrat was responsible for the internal affairs of the camp and its day to day matters, including both the provision of housing and food, and the preparation of lists for deportation. The Nazis introduced this illusory sense of self-administration to render the prisoners more controllable. SS officers, in fact, oversaw each and every action. The Ghetto commanders gave their orders orally, leaving the Jewish administrators to issue Daily Orders.

Three Jewish Elders (Judenältester) led the Ghetto self-government. Appointed by Adolf Eichmann, the first was Jakob Edelstein who served from 4 December 1941 until 27 November 1943. Arrested for falsifying deportation lists, he was sent first to the Small Fortress and then to Auschwitz. There, having been forced to watch the executions of his wife and son, on 20 June 1944, he too was shot. The second Elder, Dr Paul Eppstein was in charge from 4 December 1941 to 27 November 1943. Accused of disobeying orders, he was shot in the Small Fortress on Yom Kippur, 7 September 1944. Rabbi Dr Benjamin Murmelstein succeeded him and served until 5 May 1945 when, as the War was ending, International Red Cross delegate, Paul Dunant took over. Each of these Elders discharged the desperately challenging job of obeying Nazi orders while attending to the well-being of his fellow prisoners to the best of his ability.

The first camp commander at Terezín was Dr Siegfried Seidl. His loyalties rested with SS General Günther, Director of the Central Office for the Settling of the Jewish Question in Bohemia and Moravia (*Zentralamt für die Regelung der Judenfrage in Bohmen und Mahren*).

This organisation was answerable to the Reich Security Main Office (*Reichssicherheitshhauptamt*) in Berlin. On his desk Seidl kept a cartoon of a Jew. The caption read: "Don't get cross, always try to smile." Unable to tolerate the memory of German defeat in the First World War, this one time law student was relentlessly vindictive and brutal. Jews were no more than fodder for the gas. In his book, *Ghetto Theresienstadt*, former prisoner Zdenek Lederer records that: "when in 1942 a transport arrived from Vienna, he carefully scanned the list of names. In the end he found his prey, an aged tax collector, a certain Mueller who had once had some argument with Seidl's parents on a matter of taxation. Seidl had Mueller brought to H.Q., and saying to him "now you'll have some time to think", confined him to a cell in the basement where the poor old man was kept for three weeks on a starvation diet. When Mueller fell sick he was taken to hospital and gaoled again until diptheria and pneumonia put an end to his sufferings." (p. 74)

In 1943, Seidl was moved from Terezín to Bergen-Belsen and then to Budapest where he oversaw the deportation of 437,402 Hungarian Jews, mostly to Auschwitz. Arrested in Vienna in 1945, he was tried by the Volksgericht (Peoples' Tribunal) and hanged in February 1947.

He was succeeded in July 1943 by SS Major Anton Burger whom Eichmann trusted to carry out his orders with a scrupulousness lacking in his predecessor who had, it emerged grown rich by taking commissions for supplies reaching the Ghetto. Burger loathed the Czechs and relished the spectacle of each departing transport for the East. He enjoyed punching inmates with great force on the chin. After serving as Ghetto Kommandant, he was transferred to Berlin. After the War, Kommandant Burger escaped to West Germany and settled in Essen, where he assumed an alias and lived until his death in December 1991. His past was not exposed until three years later.

In February 1944, Burger was replaced by SS Colonel Karl Rahm, deputy head of the Prague Central Office. He was appointed to ensure the success of the *Verschönerung* (the Embellishment of the Ghetto).

After the war, Czech authorities prosecuted several members of the SS staff. Following their trials at Litomerice, Seidl and Rahm were sentenced to death, and executed. Trial transcripts show Karl Rahm trying to excuse his behaviour rather than expressing remorse. He justified himself as the passive recipient of orders which he felt compelled to carry out. Kommandant Burger escaped to West Germany, and settled in Essen, where he adopted an alias and lived until his death in December 1991.

In May 1942, the Nazi authorities in Prague ordered the Jewish communities of Bohemia and Moravia to send all their communal possessions, ranging from buckets to ritual objects, books and records, to the new Central Jewish Museum in Prague. Members of Prague's Jewish community had decided to protect the belongings of those who had been deported to the camps. For reasons that have never been disclosed, the Nazis co-operated with this aim and nearly 1,800 Torah scrolls were added to the collections of the Jewish Museum in Prague. While Magda Veselská has compellingly dismissed the idea that Hitler had planned to create a post-War Museum of Extinct Jewish Life, it is perhaps possible that he was motivated by a Nazi preoccupation with data collection, record keeping and maintaining *Alles in Ordnung*.

With this, the accustomed lives of many Czech Torah scrolls came to an end. The extermination of the Czech communities meant that, instead of fulfilling their traditional role as the most valued communal liturgical objects, to be ritually buried when worn out, Torah scrolls resurfaced as museum exhibits.

Many scrolls reached Prague with their specific accoutrements. These include a binder to prevent it from unrolling, often made from the swaddling cloth used at a boy's circumcision, and embroidered with particular iconography. The mantle to cover the scroll is also carefully decorated. Depending on the wealth of the community, silver ornaments, sometimes highly wrought, are also used. A shield hung from a chain is put over the wooden rollers that hold the scroll. A Torah pointer, the end of which is shaped like a hand with an outstretched index finger, used to help the reader follow the text, is similarly attached, and finials cover the protruding wooden roller ends.

Sefer Torah Binder, New North London Synagogue, London,
on loan from the Memorial Scrolls Trust.

When the war ended, surviving communities in Bohemia, Moravia, Slovakia, and in Prague itself, turned to the Museum for help in replacing liturgical objects. Fortunately, the Museum was able to provide some 200 scrolls. And further dramatic change lay ahead.

Along with other forms of religious life, the Communist régime which seized power in February 1948, eventually outlawed Jewish communal life. Consequently, ritual items were once more sent to the Jewish Museum in Prague. In 1950, the Museum was taken into state control. The régime forced the staff to transfer the collections to disparate sites. The removal of the scrolls to the small Michle Synagogue, 5 kilometres south of central Prague, began in 1956.

Five years later, the state forced Hana Volavková, the highly responsible Museum director, to resign. Her successor, Vilem Benda, was equally powerless to influence any major decisions taken by the Communist authorities.

While Benda appreciated the cultural and historical value of the preserved items, the Communist régime remained ambivalent, recognising that they had in hand a source of hard cash. As one scroll seemed very much like another to them, their very number made them particularly susceptible to financial ambition. Benda's protests fell on deaf ears and, in 1963, he was forced to put 1,500 Torah scrolls on the market, leaving the Jewish Museum in Prague with a mere 100 or so.

Eventually, a British art dealer, Eric Estorick, Chimen Abramsky, an expert in Judaica and consultant to Sotheby's, and philanthropist, Ralph Yablon concluded the purchase. Wrapped in polythene, the shipment of 1,564 scrolls reached London in February 1964. Rabbi Harold Reinhart agreed to store them at the Westminster Synagogue, Kent House in Knightsbridge, London. Chaired by Frank R. Waley and with Ruth Shaffer as Honorary Secretary, a committee prepared to accommodate the scrolls. A decision was made to loan as many as possible all over the world: those that could be repaired, for ritual use, and the rest for commemorative purposes.

One day in 1967, by amazing coincidence, sofer (scribe) David Brand, a new arrival from Jerusalem, knocked on the door of the Westminster Synagogue. He asked whether the Synagogue happened to have any scrolls in need of repair. The sight of three rooms stacked floor to ceiling with such scrolls exceeded all possible expectation. He had found a job that lasted 25 years.

For nearly forty years, assisted by Constance Stuart, Ruth Schaffer devotedly catalogued the scrolls and oversaw their care and distribution. When Ruth Shaffer retired in 2002, Evelyn Friedlander, author, and wife of Rabbi Albert Friedlander, Rabbi of the Westminster Synagogue, took over as one of the Trustees and Chairwoman of the committee.

Recent co-operation between what has become the Memorial Scrolls Trust in London and the Jewish Museum in Prague has contributed to the publication of the book from some of this information has been drawn: *The Second Life of the Czech Torah Scrolls*, edited by Dana and Magda Veselská. The book catalogues a celebratory exhibition of the same name held at the Westminster Synagogue, Kent House in June 2007.

Evelyn Friedlander's energy and determination resulted in the opening of a reconstructed Czech Scrolls Museum on 17 September, 2008. Now a memorial to the vanished communities, this Museum houses the scrolls that could not be distributed, and tells the remarkable story of the rescue of the entire collection.

Unrolling a Czech Torah prior to restoration, Jewish Community Centre, Prague.

Repairing the Etz Chaim of a Czech Torah, Jewish Community Centre, Prague.

GLOSSARY

BLUE ANGEL

Apfelstrudel	apple cake (Ger.)
entarteten	degenerate (Ger.)
Linzertorte	Viennese pastry (Ger.)
mein jüdischer Geliebter	my Jewish lover (Ger.)
mestizo	mixed (Span.)
métis	mixed (Fr.)
mischling	mixed race (Ger.)
Mitzvah	commandment (Heb.)
Zwetschkenstrudel	plum cake (Ger.)
כאישון עיני k'ishon einai	the apple of my eye (Heb.)

FAMILY TREE

Eretz Yisrael	Land of Israel (Heb.)
Hatikvah:	Hope, the title of the Israeli National Anthem
kehile Seiner	the Seiner family or the Seiner tribe (Yiddish)
schmattes	old clothes (Yiddish)
Seder	Passover meal (Heb.)
shicksé	non-Jewish woman (Yiddish slang)
Shul	Synagogue (Yiddish)
Simchas	joyous family events (Yiddish)
עין לציון צופיה Ayin leZion tzofi'a	Eye gazing towards Zion (Heb.) – from the Israeli National Anthem

DAMALS

5767	The year 2006/7 according to Jewish reckoning
Elul	12th month of the Jewish year (Heb.)
Heřmanův Městec	place-name in the Czech Republic
kippah	skull cap – head covering for Jewish men (Heb.)
l'chaim	to life (Heb.)
Mikveh	ritual bath (Heb.)
Minyan	quorum of 10 people needed for some Jewish prayers (Heb.)
Rosh Hashanah	New Year festival in the Jewish calendar (Heb.)

Shul	Synagogue (Yiddish)
Simcha	joyous family event (Yiddish)
tallit	prayer shawl (Heb.)

SKIN

eins zwei drei vier fünf	one two three four five (Ger.)
Hausfrauen	housewife (Ger.)
Kleiderkammer	dressing room (Ger) – where people had to undress in Terezín
Liebling	beloved (Ger.)
matka	mother (Czech)
prosím	please (Czech)
sei doch nicht so geizig	Don't be so stingy (Ger.)
Winterhilfe	winter help (Ger.) – organisation to help the elderly and poor
באמונה שלמה b'emunah sh'leimah	with perfect faith (Heb.)

THE PIOUS PLACE BY THE RIVER OHŘE

Arbeit macht frei	Work sets you free (Ger.) – written above the gates of death camps
Bar Mitzvah	Son of commandments (Heb.) – coming of age in the Jewish tradition
brachah	blessing (Heb.)
komm	come (Ger.)
Punkt	point, minute quantity (Ger.)
Sei nicht böse lach mal	Don't be angry, do laugh (Ger.)
Die Uhr tickt gut	The clock works well (Ger.) – meaning they are dying, their time is up
Volksmaterial	Folklore (Ger.)
Wissenschaft des Judentums	Jewish Studies (Ger.)
Yid	Jewish (slang, Eastern European)
כשרות Kashrut	Jewish dietary rules, foods that are suitable (Heb.)
נהר השמות n'har hashemot	a river of names (Heb.)
נזכור שארית נחלתנו nizkor sh'erit nakhalatenu	We shall remember the remnant of our people (Heb.)

GEDENKSTÄTTE

dolcemente subito	suddenly very sweetly (Italian)
einsam	lonely (Ger.)

Gedenkstätte	memorial site
gracioso	gracefully (Italian)
leicht bewegt	nimble and with movement (Ger.)
sforzando	forcefully, with attack
Unsterbliche Geliebte	immortal beloved (Ger.)

APPASSIONATA

arpeggio	broken chord (It.)
Brundibár	Children's opera by Hans Krása
Chuppah	wedding canopy (Heb.)
piano e pianissimo	quietly and very quietly (It.)
sonata apasionata	The title as it appears on the programme of Alice Sommer-Herz's concert

I SPEAK TO THE CHILD THAT I WAS

alles aus	everyone out (Ger.)
Baruch Ha Shem	Blessed be the Name
in Ordnung	in order (Ger.)
liebe Gott	dear God (Ger.)
raus:	out (Ger.)

POLITIK 3

drahoušek miláček mazlíček	Darling (Czech)
mutti	mummy (Ger.)

GAN EDEN

gan Eden	garden of Eden (Heb)
Hallel	psalms sung on Jewish Festivals

RATION

Baruch HaShem	Blessed be the Name (Heb.), an expression of thankfulness

TOMATOPHOBIA

mensch	decent human being (Yiddish)
pünktlich	punctually (Ger.)
Wassersuppe	water soup (Ger.)

FAMILY

Chanukah	Lit. dedication. An eight-day Jewish festival cele-brated in winter
Midrash	Lit. story. A story of Biblical exegesis (Heb.)
אוד מוצל מאש od mutzal m'eish	The remnant saved from the fire (Heb.)

DIES IRAE

The title is taken from a thirteenth-century Latin hymn which is part of the Roman Catholic Requiem Mass; a famous musical setting is in Verdi's *Requiem*, which was performed at Terezín.

ausgerechnet	of all things (Ger.) (used in Fritz Beda-Löhner's version of 'Yes, We Have No Bananas')
die irae dies illa	day of wrath, day of mourning (Lat.)
Dies Irae	day of wrath (Lat.)
ganzes Herz	whole heart (Ger.) (The phrase comes from Fritz Beda-Löhner's libretto for Léhar's operetta, 'The Land of Smiles', in which Richard Tauber starred).
Glück und Komfort	Bliss and comfort: German slogan used during the Embelishment.
Judenaleteste	Jewish Elder (Ger.)
jüdische	Jewish (Ger.)
Jüdisches kindchen	little jewish children (Ger.)
meine Mutter	my mother (Ger.)
die Ringstraße	a street in Vienna
die schwarze Hexe	the black witch (Ger.)
Sieg Heil	hail victory/we will win (Nazi greeting, Ger.)
Teufelskind	devil's child (Ger.)
Wehrmacht	German Army (Ger.)

KOBLIHY

ausgezeichnetes Material	excellent material (Ger.)
koblihy	doughnuts (Czech)
l'chaim	to life (Heb).
Lohengrin	Arthurian opera by Wagner
Pfannkuchen	doughnuts (Ger.)

ACKNOWLEDGEMENTS

Jane and Marion would like to thank all those who have contributed to *Faces in the Void* especially those who so generously took the time and the trouble to share their memories.

The project has been generously sponsored by: Helen and Ira Nordlicht (USA), Beth Shalom Reform Synagogue (Cambridge), Cambridge Jewish Residents' Association, Michaelhouse Centre (Cambridge) and the Sir Halley Stewart Trust.

They would like to thank the Czech Centre and in particular, Evelyn Friedlander and Michael Heppner at the Czech Memorial Scrolls Trust.

In the Czech Republic, Leo Pavlat, Director of the Jewish Museum in Prague, Dana and Magda Veselská, Noemi Holeková, Jarmila Reichentalvá, Helena Becková, Alexander Putik, Silvie Wittmann and Petr Brod were ceaselessly helpful. We would like to thank the Jewish Museum, Prague, the Jewish Community of Prague, the Federation of Jewish Communities in the Czech Republic and the Terezín Memorial and the officials in the Town Hall in Pardubice.

Margrit Rechner has given great help from America.

Jane would also like to thank Ian Bolton and Adrian Newman at AVMG, Cambridge, and Victoria Bursa, Alison Hennegan, Linda Hepner, Helmut Jedliczka, Eva Kandler, Dr Diana Lipton, Kay Lacey, Myrtle and Peter Popper, Dr Anne Summers, John Thirlwell, Edith Weisz, and in particular, Dr Avra Cohn and Angela Thirlwell.

BIBLIOGRAPHY

Of the books we have continuously consulted we must single out:

Anon., *Lidice* (Dokumenty Doby, Praha, 1945)

Bar, Arthus, *50 Jahre Hak oah 1909–1959* (Verlagskomitee Hakoah Tel Aviv, 1959)

Barkow, Ben and Leist, Klaus (eds), *As If It Were Life: A WWII Diary from the Theresienstadt Ghetto* (Palgrave Macmillan, 2009)

Carsten, F. L., *Fascist Movements in Austria* (Sage Publications Ltd., 1977)

Chládková, Ludmila, *The Terezín Ghetto* (Jitka Kejřová, V RÁJI Publishers, 2005)

Denscher, Barbara and Peschina, Helmut, *No Land of Smiles* (place, publisher and date unspecified)

Fiedler, Jiří, *Jewish Sights of Bohemia and Moravia* (Sefer, 1991)

Gilman, Sander L. and Zipes, Jack, *The Companion to Jewish Writing and Thought 1066–1996* (Yale, 1997)

Huppert, Jehuda and Drori, Hana, *Theresienstadt, a Guide* (Vitalis, 2005)

Kieval, Hillel J. *The Making of Czech Jewry* (OUP, 1988)

Lederer, Zdenek, *Ghetto Theresienstadt* (Edward Goldston and Son Ltd., London, 1953)

Ruzicková, Renata; Langova, Albeta; and Bartos, Strepan, *Traces of the Jews in the Pardubice Region* (Pardubicky Kraj, 2006)

Stone, Dan, *Constructing the Holocaust* (Vallentine Mitchell, 2003)

Veselská, Dana and Veselská, Magda (eds), *The Second Life of the Czech Torah Scrolls* (Jewish Museum, Prague, 2006)

Wood, Ean, *The Josephine Baker Story* (Sanctuary Publishing, 2000).

(Following three pages) Two views of the Memorial by Marie Uchytilová to the Child-Victims of the War, Lidice.

149